MORETON WIRRAL

A Pictorial History

Volume 2

by

Frank Biddle & Alan Fellowes

STILL ABLE TO SIT UP AND TAKE
NOURISHMENT ·

AT MORETON.

First published 1993 by Countyvise Limited, 1 & 3 Grove Road, Rock Ferry, Birkenhead, Wirral, Merseyside L42 3XS, and Metropolitan Borough of Wirral, Central Library, Borough Road, Birkenhead, Wirral L41 2XB.

Copyright © Frank Biddle and Alan Fellowes, 1993.

ISBN 0 907768 59 8 Countyvise Limited.

ISBN 0 904582 16 7 Metropolitan Borough of Wirral, Central Library.

Photoset and printed by Birkenhead Press Limited, 1 & 3 Grove Road, Rock Ferry, Birkenhead, Merseyside L42 3XS.
Front cover designed by Michelle Smith.

The top picture is of the unveiling of the Wallasey sign on the Moreton/Saughall massie bridge by the Mayor or Wallasey, Dr. John McMillan. He is the man wearing the top hat, just left of centre - the date being April 1st, 1928.

The picture below is of the old Coach and Horses Bowling Green where Lennons supermarket, later Gateway, now Solo supermarket is. Behind the bowling green is Briscoe's farm house. The picture dates from the early 1950's.

The top picture dates from 1930. The main interest is of the shops on the right - the first one was a tool shop owned by Mr. Whitthread and the last one on the corner of Chadwick Street was a newsagents owned and run by Mr Hopkins.

The picture below was taken in 1960. The shops stood where Kwik Save's old shop now stands and the other shops. They were pulled down in the early 1960's. The shops were run by firstly Owens, the greengrocers, then Sharps, shoe repairers, a cake and sweet shop, then Faulkner's the Morton Poultry Supplies who moved to the new shops by Alwyn Gardens, then to where it is now at the Cross, now called the pet shop. The other shop was Strodes the fish shop. Mr Stroude also had another small shop by the roundabout at the Cross.

The picture above is of Hoylake Road looking towards Moreton Cross and Birkenhead, and dates from the early 1900's. The first building is a barn, the second is Piggot's farm and was sited roughly where the Gas Show Room and Rumbelows are now. The next building on the corner of Digg Lane was owned by Job Thomas and was pulled down in the early 1980's. Piggot's farm was used by Percy Mortimer, see picture below, to start his grocery business. the people in the picture below are Mr and Mrs Mortimer and Eileen Wilson - the little boy is her brother. As can be seen in the picture, Mr. Mortimer later added a bay window to display his goods. When Danny Evans took the shop over in the 1930's he had the window removed, leaving it flat. Mr Mortimer had a purpose-build shop built next door to sell meccano, Dinky toys and bicycles, later extended and expanding to sell prams and baby goods. The end of the building was rented by Mr Chalmers, the shoe repairer. When the building was pulled down in 1973, the toy department moved over the road to the corner of Rosslyn Drive. They later sold out to Keithley's. The pram and baby part moved to Upton Road, to where 'In-Stitches' used to be.

The top picture, dating from the 1940's, is of the line of shops from Holt Avenue to Rosslyn Drive. The first part of the picture shows Holt Buildings, which was pulled down in the early 1960's. The shops were occupied by Birds, the drapers, (they also sold men's shoes and clothing - the entrance being in Holt Avenue). The next shop was J W Lee's, a shoe shop, then Frazer's, a green grocers. Above these shops was a Billiard Room and one room was used by the Conservative Club and for Parish Council meetings. The building that replaced these was Barclays Bank and Lavell's, the newsagents (now Martins). Lavells started off as Sainsbury's. The rest of the shops are still there. One was the Willow Farm Dairy; a hairdressers owned by Mrs Mary Holt; Woodfield Cooke (a chemist), who always had a grey enamel weighing machine outside. The end shop was Lunts, the bread shop, and the only shop still unchanged is M.A.N.W.E.B. The picture below dates from the early 1940's. The following are the occupants of the shops between Joan Avenue and Francis Avenue. Firstly came the Paint Shop owned by Frank Ewing, then McMillan & Co., an off licence shop which it still is today, and then Thomas, the signwriter. Next came William Camm, the butcher, then E. L. Fellowes the wireless & Electrical shop (now the Lee Ho Chinese Restaurant), Hopwood, the chemist, now Maxwell's the ladies hairdressers and finally the last one was an ironmongers, owned by Robert Murray, and is now a launderette.

Both pictures on this page date from 1927. The top one is of Borrowdale Road, once Churchill Road. The bungalow on the right is the only building still standing, all the others have been pulled down and rebuilt.

The picture below is of Meadowbrook Road. The house in the picture was a grocers shop until the 1940's and is one of many in Moreton that have changed from shops to private homes. In Borrowdale Road there is a short terrace on the right hand side - three of these were shops, one being a grocers shop, another a bicycle shop and the other a ladies hairdressers. The house and bungalow on the right of the bottom picture are still there.

The top picture dates from 1953. the large building on the left was known as Valder's Cycle Shop until the 1960's. Since then it has been a television shop, a hairdressers and a double glazing shop. You will see that there are no houses on either side of the shop, these came later during the late 1950's/early 1960's.

The picture below is looking towards Saughall Massie and was taken in 1930. You can just make out The Grange and Jordan's farm on the right, in the distance. On the left of the picture was a cricket pitch, the Grange Hotel now stands on this spot and was built in the early 1930's.

The top picture dates from the early 1930's and shows Saughall Massie bridge. This was the Wallasey boundary until it was extended to include Saughall Massie. On the left of the picture is Charlton's Fish and Chip shop. It lasted for about 30 years and closed down in 1962. It later became a garden centre for a short while and is now a glaziers. The short row of shops on the other side of the bridge were built in the mid 1920's. The furthest one away has always been the Saughall Bridge Post Office. The next one was the Wallasey Corporation Gas Service Shop and used to sell coke at the back of the shop until the late 1950's. The nearest two shops were owned by Mrs. Laidlaw, one being a Wine shop closing in the 1950's and the other was a Cake Shop which had a big extension on the back to be used for functions. It was used during the wartime as a British Restaurant.

In 1954 Mrs Laidlaw sold the premises to the Hale family and they ran it as a cake shop until the late 1980's. Both the wine and cake shops are now vacant.

The picture below as taken in 1927 when the last of the shops were being built. The first shop was a sweet shop and was pulled down in the middle 1980's to accommodate the present Caravan Company. The other shops have been many things over the years. Mr Speakman started his cycle shop in No. 138 and later moved to Saughall Massie.

Hoylake Road, Moreton.

The two pictures on this page are of "The Grange". It was situated on the corner of Saughall Massie Road and Hoylake Road where the shops are now. It gave its name to the public house on the corner of Acton Lane and Hoylake Road. The roads on the "Grange Estate" were named after parts of the original "Grange Estate", namely: The Paddock, Orchard Grange, Coppice Grange. It was built in the late 1800's for the Griffith family who dealt in horse transport. It was used as a summer residence only and had a large staff to run it, as can be seen in the picture below. During the winter a family were kept on to take care of the place. It was pulled down in the middle 1930's. The Griffith family were staunch members of the Presbyterian Church and many garden parties were held there. Many local families worked for them. Mr & Mrs Mountain were the caretakers all the year round, just to name a few. Old Tom Jordan married one of the maids (the grandfather of Tony Jordan who represented his country playing badminton).

Both pictures on this page are of Acton Lane. The top one, taken in 1927, shows the bottom part where the Arrowebrook runs along the side of the lane amongst the trees - you can see the back of the bungalows in Meadowbrook Road.

The picture below , taken in the late 1930's, shows Acton Lane after the building was finished, although the road surface was still to be done. The Grange Estate was built by Tate, Pumfort & Doughty and Gledhill between 1931 and 1937.

The pictures on this page show two of the shops where the Grange used to be - both pictures were taken in the 1930's. The top picture, taken in 1933, shows Flo James, Mrs. Hughes and Dolly, (the delivery boy was Eric) outside Mrs. Hughes' shop.

The picture below shows the W. Davies, Saughall and Carr Dairy. It later became known as Wrights Dairy until it was bought by Michael who turned it into a Fish & Chip shop in 1966 and it still is owned by Michael. The man on the left of the door below is Mr. Davies.

The top picture dates from the late 1930's and it shows the Hoylake Road being widened. This road was commonly known as the Meols Stretch and it ran between Saughall Road and Meols Station. Jordan's farm can just be seen on the left and on the right are the shops that belong to the Grange Estate. Going back over the road again, there is, at the side of Jordan's farm (also known as Millhouse Farm), a lane called Millhouse Lane. Both the farm and the lane got their names from the mill that stood on the corner of Acton Lane. The mill was owned by the Vyner family and was rented out at £6 per year. The mill was made of wood and stood until 1870. It was then left empty and quickly began to fall down. It was soon dismantled, leaving no trace of its origins. The last miller was Mr Richard Hale.

Below is Jordan's farm taken in 1950. It was built in the late 1790's and pulled down in the 1950's. It stood on the corner of Millhouse Lane and Hoylake Road and was run as a small-holding which ran down to Arrowe Brook. A garage and petrol filling station are on the site of the old farm, which was owned by the Jordan family until recently. It was called Millhouse Farm but was also an ale house for a short time in the early 1800's.

The top picture dating from 1910 shows Salisbury's cottage. It was one of two and to get to the second one you went up an alleyway at the back. The cottages were built in the late 1790's and pulled down in 1931. The electric sub-station and the extension on the Saughall Hotel now occupy the site. The people in the top picture are Mr & Mrs George and Alice Salisbury. the front cottage was one of the original Inn's in the village and still had a vat in the back of the building when it was pulled down. There was also an iron ring in the front wall for horses to be tethered to.

The picture below, taken in the late 1920,s, shows the cottage above and the old Saughall Hotel, parts of which date from the 18th century. There has been an ale house or an inn, if not on that site, certainly in the village from the middle of the 14th century. In the Licensing Session for Wirral in 1561, a Mr Thomas Smythe of Saugon-massie was recorded as an Ale House Keeper. The hotel has been greatly extended since this picture was taken. The group of people in the picture are a Canadian family on holiday.

Both pictures show Saughall Massie village. The top one looking from West Kirby Road dates from 1910 and the bottom one looking from Saughall Road, dates from the 1900's. The top picture shows the Birkenhead Volunteers marching through the village. They left Grange Road West Drill hall, Birkenhead, in the morning and did a route march through Greasby, Saughall Massie, Upton and returned to the Drill Hall. A white house seen in the middle of the top picture was known as the White House and had an interesting history. It was possibly the third or fourth house on that site. The first one dates from 1323 and was built for Lucy de Salghal (wife of Robert de Salghal). It was pulled down in 1690 and rebuilt for the Saughall family. It then lay empty for many years and was in a very bad state of repair when it was bought by a Mr Robert Blackburn Hill and pulled down again because of its condition and rebuilt in 1953. There is a house plate on the present building showing the names of past owners L dE S 1323 S 1690 RBH 1953.

The bottom pictures shows Mr Lester, the local butcher. Just behind him is "Ivy Cottage".

The picture above shows "The Cottage" and "Ash Tree Cottage". The building was originally divided into barns and stables and was converted into two cottages in the late 1790's. "The Cottage" was rented by the Davies family from 1790 until 1900. The Boardman family then moved in and it is still occupied by them. "Ash Tree Cottage" occupies the right side half of the building, with the stables on the end. The stables were pulled down in the early 1970's. The first family to live there was the Smith family, followed by the Broster family and then the Burrows family. The Thomas family are the present owners. (The photograph was taken from Barnacre Lane (its original name was Banakers Lane). The picture below shows Saughall Massie Road bridge. On the far side of the bridge on the right, can be seen the horse mounting steps and stile. On the near side of the bridge, there was a watering place for cattle.

THE BRIDGE SAUGHALL MASSIE.

"The Unique Series".

The picture above dates from the 1920's and is of Saughall Massie Road looking towards Overchurch and Upton. The area was known as "Fairyland". Below shows "Ivy Cottage" built in 1690 for Arthur and Ellen Godwyn as can be seen on the date stone. It has been extended many times over the years and buttresses had also been added to prevent tilting. This work was done in the late 1890's. "Ivy Cottage" is one of the few thatched cottages left on the Wirral. The Broster family have lived in it for many generations now. The cottage was split in two at one time, with two toilets, and was turned into a single dwelling in the late 1930's.

The picture below shows Whitehouse Farm. It was run by the Mutch family until the mid to late 1940's. and then lay empty for a while, until it was bought by Mr. Wilding in the early 1950's. He then had it knocked down and built the bungalow call "Manyana" on the back garden of the farm. This photograph was taken in the early 1920's and is looking towards the village on the West Kirby Road. The top picture was taken about the same time and shows the village with Whitehouse Farm just out of the picture - as can be seen if you look at the wall on the immediate left and check with picture below.

The two pictures on this page are of Toll Bar Cottage. It was built in 1840 as a place where tolls were collected on that road - the road was called turnpike Road - it is now known as the Meols Stretch. Several families lived in the cottage over the years including the Ennion and Meadows families. It was finally pulled down in the late 1930's when the road was widened.

The top picture was taken just before it was pulled down and the bottom picture was taken in the 1920's. This picture was taken from Garden Hay Rd looking across to Carr Lane. The cottage was also used a a farm workers' cottage.

The top picture shows Stanley's Farm (Carr lane Farm). The picture below shows cows in Carr Lane, with the back of Stanley's farm on the right - the cattle probably belonged to the farm. It was bombed in the war and the house and farm buildings were destroyed.

The above picture is of Carr Hall Farm (Smith's Farm). This picture was taken shortly before it was pulled down (see page 4, Vol. 1) in the 1960's.

Below is Brookfield Farm just before it was pulled down in the 1960's. It was situated on the left of Saughall Massie Road, just over the bridge when going from Saughall Massie Village towards Upton. It was run by Bob Coxon and his family, and later occupied by the Heavysage and Robinson families.

The picture above is of Diamond Farm built in 1728 for Thomas and Elizabeth Harrison as can be seen on the date stone. It was built onto a 14th century crofters cottage that was thatched. The barn and other out buildings also dated from that time and were also thatched. The original buildings were made of sandstone and hand-made bricks were used when the buildings were raised and extended. You can still see the original buildings today. It was run by the Wilkinson family for two hundred years until 1961 and is now run by the Reed family. The picture that dates from 1910 shows old Mr Wilkinson feeding his horse called Prince. On the farm house just above Mr Wilkinson, you can see the date stone between two small windows. The farm servants quarters were housed in the roof space and the small windows were the only means of light. That part of the roof was lowered in 1961.

Below shows "The Elms" Farm. It was built in 1670 and was run by the Brosters family until 1972. Mainly as a pig farm the To,pkinson family bought it and made the alterations and extensions and then sold it. It is now owned by the Rozario family and has been extended and is now almost unrecognisable. The man in the carriage was Mr. Lester, a Hoylake butcher who used to deliver the meat to the village. The picture dates from the early 1900's, its original name was The White Cottage.

The top picture shows the Carr Lane Railway Crossing and house. the house was built when the railway was laid in the 1860's and was pulled down in the 1960's. It was replaced with a dormer bungalow. The gates are operated by hand and people wishing to cross the railway line had to ring a bell to call the keeper to open the gates. The top picture dates from the early 1900's. The one below dates from 1938 and shows Mrs Eliza Wharton and her daughter Violet operating the signals. the signal box stood outside the front door and still does. The Wharton family looked after the crossing from the late 1920's until 1960 when the birkenhead family replaced them. The present gate-keeper is Mrs Susan Deakin and possibly the last, with the modernisation of the crossing. Several bad accidents happened over the years, one notable one occurred on the last weekend in January, 1938, when a Mr and Mrs Ditchfield where knocked down and killed. The crossing was closed permanently on the 1st December 1993 and is now only used by farmers with special permission

Lingham Farm was built in 1800. It was then divided into two cottages which were thatched until they were burnt down in the late 1800's. The farm was then rebuilt and made into a large farmhouse, the Stanley family being the first tenants. The Dodd family took over later, through marriage, and stayed there until 1947 when the Meadows brother bought it and turned it into a market garden, and they in turn ran it until 1980. It was then taken over by Mr. J. P Biddle and Son and was returned to farming again, growing potatoes, hay and oats, and having up to 100 beef cattle.

The top picture dating from 1953 shows the fields and farmhouse when it was run as a market garden by the Meadows family, the house is now owned by Mr & Mrs Hoane and the farm building has now also been converted into a home. The picture below taken in 1880 shows Mrs. Stanley feeding the hens.

The picture above is of Lingham bridge across the River Birket. The old bridge was demolished in the late 1950's when the river was widened and the banks were shored up and the mill stones were removed. The picture was taken in 1906 and shows two thatched corn stacks. It is said that there were plans to build a watermill there but this idea fell through as a dam would not have been allowed to be built because of flooding the fields towards Meols.

Below is Lingham Cottage in 1880 which was run as a small holding. The third building along, with the man standing outside, is thatched. It was extended sometime in the late 1890's to give two bedrooms upstairs that were accessible through a trap door. The cottage was built in the late 1700's; the Stott family live there now.

The 'Emblematic' was built in 1873 by Joseph Shepherd & Co., in Low Building Yard, Whitehaven. It was 53 feet 10-1/2 inches long and 15 feet 7 inches wide. Its tonnage was 34-1/2 tons and its hull was built of pitch pine and had oak ribs. She was possibly named after the 1864 Grand National winner and was bought by James Eccles in 1874 for £750. She was a fishing smack. Hoylake was then a small fishing village with a fleet of forty or so fishing vessels, although primarily fishing vessels, they would be used for carrying coal and many other things. The picture above, on the left, shows the Emblematic being unloaded in 1879. The picture below shows the crew on board the Emblematic; they were from left to right:- William Eccles senior, William Eccles junior, Joseph Eccles and 'Skitter' Bird.

The Emblematic was at anchor in the Hoyle lake and in January 1883 a storm blew up and she lost her anchor and was driven along the shore and into the footing of the embankment at Moreton, half was between Dovepoint and Leasowe Lighthouse. The embankment, as in 1976 when the boat was uncovered, was being rebuilt. It is said that the workers were given just 24 hours to get the boat out. They tried to move it in the first tide but it was just too well embedded in the wall so they stripped the boat of everything that would move and she was literally built into the embankment.

The top picture shows the Emblematic being built into the wall in 1883. Below can be seen the outline of the boat in the embankment in 1953.

The top picture on this page taken in November 1976, shows the Emblematic being made ready to float her out when the tide came in. In the bottom picture you can see that it is just starting to float. The men made a small channel at the base of the wall so the boat would not have to be lifted. After 83 years embedded in the embankment, it was remarkable that she could still float and it must have been a wonderful sight.

Many families had their photographs taken when they came to Moreton Shore, whether it was for the day or the week, and in some cases, for the entire season from march through to November. Families closed their homes and one member of the family would return home once a week or maybe once a month, to check that everything was alright and check on their mail. Many photographs has a two-fold use:- On the reverse side it was marked out to be used as a postcard. The photographs were taken by Mr G E Mills, the top one shows him photographing another photographer, who is most likely a Mr Wilkinson, who lived in Wallasey. Mr & Mrs Mills came from Liverpool, another one was a Mr S J Carter from Chester. The Liverpool Photographic Club also came to Moreton and E. R. J. of Greasby, just to metion a few of the many who we are indebted to, as otherwise a book like this would not be possible.

The bottom picture shows two young men having a 'greasy-pole' pillow fight, cheered on by the crowd. Both photographs/postcards date from the late 1900's.

LEASOWE CAMP SPORTS
BANK HOLIDAY AUG 1908

The Sports Days on Leasowe Common (now known as Moreton Common or Moreton Shore) were highly organised affairs. By the time the picture above was taken in 1906, although they held Sports Days at Easter, the big one was always on the August Bank Holiday (which was then the first Monday in August, not the last as is now). The Sports Day was held on Moreton Common opposite Bankfield House and Stone House.

The picture below is dated 1908. On the facing page, the top picture dates from 1911 and the bottom one is also from the same period.

Both pictures on this page date from 1911 and show the sports Committee in the top one and the Officials in the bottom one. The next four pages shows a programme dated August 13th, 1914. It was the last Sports Day to be held for five years as war was declared with Germany on that day; a rather sad but happy day as things turned out.

Leasowe Camping Association.

ELEVENTH ANNUAL GYMKHANA, AUGUST 3, 1914.

Patrons:
Alderman A. Goodwin.   D. J. Clarke, Esq., T.C.   J. A. Kerr, Esq.

President: Richard Ledsom, Esq.

Vice-Presidents: Messrs. G. H. Pickering, A. Irving, Step. Byrne, I. Taylor, Roger Halsall, Mott Cohen, and A. W. Ball.

Honorary Members: Messrs. Arthur Harrison, Harry Tindall, Tom Kenny, Llew Lewis, B. Ogden and J. Joplin.

Judges: Messrs. H. Monk (Chief), W. Delaney, P. D. Evans, E. May, P. Ainslie, A. W. Ball, S. Sheen and A. Marshall.

Starter: Harry Tindall.   **Handicapper:** Mott Cohen.   **Clerk-of-Course:** W. H. Boulton.

Committee and Stewards: Messrs. A. Anderton, T. H. Beacall, H. Curran, W. B. Clarke, G. Cregeen, W. L. Daniels, J. Dawson, W. Holyoake, J. Jones, F. W. Jones, F. Lamb, J. Love, J. Lowe, D. Lewis, H. Lewis, W. J. Moore, L. McConomy, A. McGee, C. E. Overton, J. Percival, B. Robinson, T. Rule, Jos. Schorah, W. J. Thompson, J. Perry, Senr. Chas. J. Fleming (Press Steward).

Hon. Treasurer: Len Robinson.   **Hon. Secretary:** Arthur E. May.

Programme and Time Table.

TENNIS TOURNAMENT (Doubles).
Winners—1 Box Cigars, presented by Mr. W. Hale.
" " Mr. S. Morris.

GOLF TOURNAMENT (Singles)
1st Prize—Selected.
2nd " "

9-30 a.m.—CROQUET GOLF TOURNAMENT—Ladies and Gentlemen.
1st Prize (Ladies), Case Afternoon Tea Knives, presented by Mrs. Richard Ledsom.
2nd Prize (Ladies), Cake Stand, presented by Mr. and Mrs. Jones.
3rd Prize (Ladies), Pair Vases, presented by P.D.E.
4th Prize (Ladies), Pair Pictures, presented by Miss Scholfield.
1st Prize (Gents), Box 100 Cigars, presented by Mr. J. Musker.
2nd Prize (Gents), Oak Biscuit Barrel, presented by Mr. J. A. Kerr.
3rd Prize (Gents), Leather Collar Box, presented by Mr. and Mrs. Beacall.
4th Prize (Gents), Cake Dish, presented by L.C.A.
Prize for Girl under 16—E.P.N.S Egg Cruet, presented by Mrs. Banner.
Prize for Boy under 16—Barometer, presented by L.C.A.

11-0 " 40 YARDS FLAT RACE—Children under 8 years.
1st Prize (Girls), Teddy Bear, presented by Mr. A. Marshall.
2nd Prize " Tennis Racquet, presented by L.C.A.
3rd Prize " Box Oil Colours " "
1st Prize (Boys), Box Paints, presented by L.C.A.
2nd Prize " Golf Club " "
3rd Prize " Clock-work Boat " "
And six other Prizes for both Boys and Girls.

11-15 " 50 YARDS FLAT RACE—Boys under 12 years.
1st Prize, Enlargement of Winner, presented by Mr. Wilkinson.
2nd Prize, Cricket Bat, presented by Mrs. I. Taylor.
3rd Prize, Set of Wickets, presented by a Friend.

11-30 " 50 YARDS FLAT RACE—Girls under 12 years.
1st Prize, Coloured Miniature of Winner in Locket, presented by Mr. G. Ernie Mills.
2nd Prize, Glove Box, presented by L.C.A.
3rd Prize, School Companion, presented by L.C.A.

11-45 " 80 YARDS FLAT RACE—Boys under 15 years.
1st Prize, Medal, presented by Mr. Phil-de-Freece.
2nd Prize, Pair Hair Brushes, presented by L.C.A.
3rd Prize, Pencil Case, presented by L.C.A.
4th Prize, Jam Dish, " "

12-0 noon—80 YARDS FLAT RACE—Girls under 15 years.
1st Prize, Tea Service, presented by Mrs. Bostock.
2nd Prize, E.P.N.S. Honey Jar, presented by Mrs. E. May.
3rd Prize, Brush and Comb Case, presented by L.C.A.
4th Prize, Trinket Glass, presented by L.C.A.

1-30 p.m.—FINAL Children under 8 years.

1-45 " " Boys " 12 "

2-0 " " Girls " 12 "

2-15 " " Boys " 15 "

2-30 " " Girls " 15 "

2-45 " 100 YARDS FLAT RACE (HANDICAP)—Members only.
1st Prize, E.P.N.S. Egg Cruet, presented by the Gourock Rope Work Co., Ltd.
2nd Prize, Case Fish Carvers, presented by Mr. Jos. Schorah, senr.
3rd Prize, Brass Smokers Set, presented by Mr. and Mrs. John Jones.
4th Prize, Pair Photo Frames, presented by Mrs. Jos. Schorah.
5th Prize, Pocket Wallet, presented by the L.C.A.

32

3-0 p.m.—EGG AND SPOON RACE—Ladies.

1st Prize, E.P.N.S. Sugar Basin and Sifter, presented by Mrs. Austin.
2nd Prize, Fire Screen, presented by Mr. J. A. Kerr.
3rd Prize, E.P.N.S. Jam Dish, presented by Mr. & Mrs. L. McConomy.
4th Prize, Pair Pictures, presented by The Co-operative Society.
5th Prize, E.P.N.S. Butter Dish, presented by Mr. Austin Delaney.

3-15 „ TORTOISE RACE ON BICYCLES (40 yards)—Last in wins—Members only.

1st Prize, Travelling Rug, presented by Messrs. J. Langdon & Sons.
2nd Prize, Brass Ink Stand, presented by Mr. W. H. Smith.
3rd Prize, Case Military Brushes, presented by Mr. J. Wharton.
4th Prize, Vacuum Flask, presented by L.C.A.

3-30 „ HALF-MILE FLAT RACE (HANDICAP)—Members only.

1st Prize, Pair Bronze Figures, presented by Mr. Joplin's Tent.
2nd Prize, Silver-mounted Umbrella, presented by Messrs. Job Thomas & Sons.
3rd Prize, E.P.N.S. Cruet, presented by Mr. Roger Halsall.
4th Prize, Brass Jug, presented by Mr. and Mrs. John Jones.
5th Prize presented by "A Friend."

3-45 „ FLOWER POT RACE (20 yards).

1st Prize, Silver Cigarette Case, presented by Mr. Mott Cohen.
2nd Prize, Case Carvers, presented by Mr. W. J. Thompson.
3rd Prize, Alarum Clock, presented by Mr. and Mrs. Geo. Smith.
4th Prize, Rug, presented by Mr. Jones, Tithebarn Street.

4-0 „ NEEDLE THREADING RACE—Ladies and Members.

1st Prize (Ladies), Silver-mounted Umbrella, presented by Messrs. Daniels and Cregeen.
2nd Prize „ Brass Flower Pot Stand, presented by L.C.A.
3rd Prize „ Morocco Satchel, presented by Mr. and Mrs. A. W. Ball.
1st Prize (Gents), Despatch Case, presented by Mr. H. Lewis' Tent.
2nd Prize „ Intermittent Alarum Clock, presented by Mr. and Mrs. J. Terry, senr,
3rd Prize „ Brass Pipe Rack, presented by Mr. J. Bennett.

4-15 „ HAM SLICING COMPETITION—Members only.

Prize—The Ham.

4-30 „ TILTING THE BUCKET COMPETITION.

Winners—Barometers.

4-45 „ 80 YARDS FLAT RACE—Ladies.

1st Prize, Hand-painted Cushion, presented by Mrs. Monk.
2nd Prize, Case Afternoon Tea Spoons, presented by Mr. and Mrs. A. W. Ball.
3rd Prize, E.P.N.S. Butter Dish, presented by Mr. and Mrs. W. Delaney.
4th Prize, E.P.N.S. Cruet, presented by Mr. W. J. Moore.
5th Prize, Pair Flower Vases, presented by L.C.A.

5-0 „ OBSTACLE RACE—Members only.

1st Prize, Salad Bowl, presented by Mr. Richard Ledsom.
2nd Prize, Eight-day Clock, presented by Mr. A. Irving.
3rd Prize, Silver Match Box, presented by Mrs. Mott Cohen.
4th Prize, Breakfast Cruet, presented by Messrs. Phillips (Lime Street).

5-15 „ RELAY RACE (Teams of Four)—Members only.

Electro-plated Cup, presented by Mr. R. Towers, Junr. *(To be held by winning team for one year).*
4 Silver Sovereign Cases, presented by Sec. and Treas. Tent.

5-30 „ PILLOW FIGHT—Members only.

1st Prize, Case Razors, presented by Mr. H. Curran's Tent.
2nd Prize, Silver-mounted Umbrella, presented by Mr. Joe Bell.
3rd Prize, Pair Bronze Flower Pots, presented by Mr. and Mrs. J. Love.
4th Prize, Clock, presented by Mr. P. Ainslie.

5-45 „ BAND BOYS' RACE (80 yards).

1st Prize, Gold-centre Medal. 2nd Prize, Silver Medal. Prizes presented by L.C.A.

6-0 „ BOY SCOUTS' RACE (100 yards).

1st Prize, Watch, presented by Alderman A. Goodwin. 2nd Prize, Medal, presented by Mr. Richard Ledsom.

The Committee desire to thank all Contributors for their kind support.

Selections of Music will be rendered during the Afternoon by the Albert Memorial Industrial School Band.

Prize-winners in Members' races must produce their Membership Cards to the Hon. Secretary before receiving the Prize.
No Competitor to win more than one First Prize (Relay and Tilting the Bucket excepted).

The Judges' decision in all cases to be final.

ENTRANCE FEE for each Event THREEPENCE.   Children ONE PENNY.

Mr. A. ROGERS, Photographer, will take a series of Photos. of the Sports during the afternoon, and same may be purchased from the Hon. Secretary on and after August 9th.

A GRAND DANCE will be held in the City Caterers' Pavilion from 7-30 p.m. to 12 o'clock. Madame Clough's Band. Programmes SIXPENCE each.

Programmes can be had from the Hon. Secretary.

NOTE.—The Last Trains to Birkenhead Park and James Street, 11-11 p.m.   To Seacombe, 10-41 p.m.

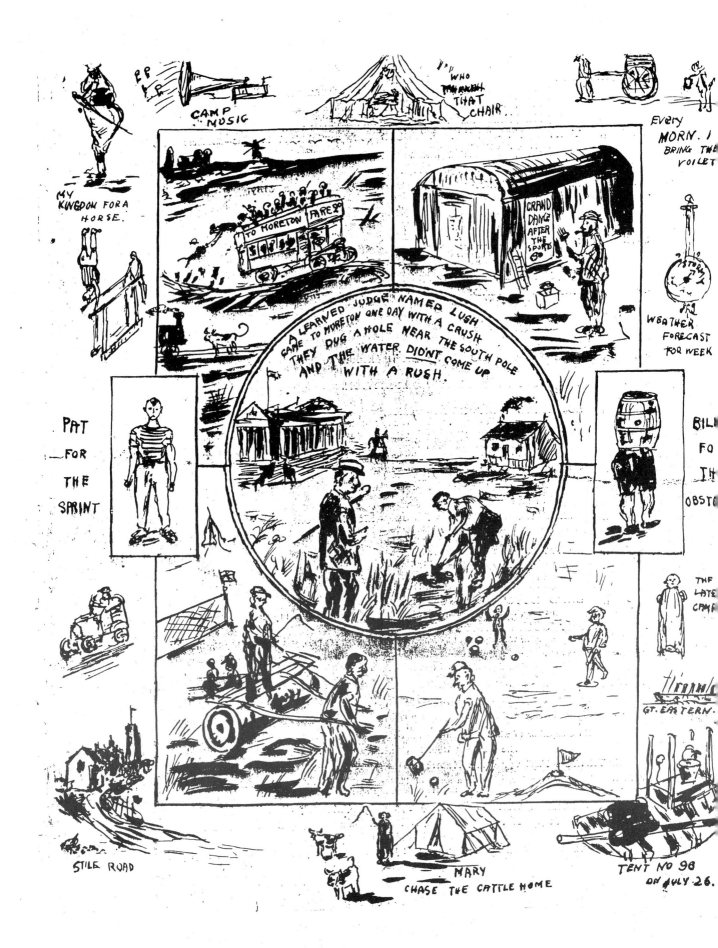

The top picture is showing Father Berry's Holiday Home for Orphaned Boys. It lasted for about fifteen years from the 1920's to the 1930's. The boys were supplied with new clothes on arrival - these clothes being supplied by the Liverpool Police.

The bottom picture is showing the Albert memorial Orphanage Brass Band. The instruments were all second-hand, having been bought from the Moreton Brass Band on its breakup. (see page 94). the band only lasted for five or six years before moving to Liverpool.

Both these pictures date from 1953 showing the short stretch of road to the embankment and looking back to the top of Pasture Road. There were six small cafes and stalls, now there is only one. There was also a black hut on the left of the picture, owned by Mr. Martindale, where deck chairs could be hired. This finally disappeared in the late 1950's. the cafe on the right at the back, was run by the Welligan family.

Both pictures on this page were taken from the roof of the lighthouse in 1926. The bottom picture shows to what extent the caravans and tents stretched. On the right of the picture are the Fellowship Fields, in the middle Pasture Farm and in the distance, on the left, can be seen Thom's Field half way down Ditton Lane on the right hand side. These were the last caravans to be cleared away - some of them lasting until the early 1950's. following is a list of the dwellings that were condemned. The owners were given Clearance Notices under a Ministry of Health Order in 1948.

Bella vista Road - 1|) Hazeldean 2) Bethany) 3) The Gables 4) the Poplars 5) Highfield 6) Mayville 7) Clintonville 8) Beaulah 9) The Haven 2, Seafield Road, 10 Seafield Road, 6 Homefield, Seafield Road, 7 Norma's cottage, Seafield Road.

1. Franklyn Villa, 2 Calda Villa, 3 Oak Lodge, 4 rose Mount, ALL IN Sand Dune Road

Birket Road - 22 Birket road 2) Wyanora, 3) Williamsville, 4) The Poplars.

In all a total of 22. the people were to be re-housed in existing houses and flats in Moreton until newly built houses became available.

The picture above was taken in the early 1930's and shows part of leasowe looking towards Wallasey Village. At the bottom of the picture, on the left, is Leasowe Castle and on the right ins the New Brighton Rugby Club, founded in 1875. The first playing ground was in Rake Lane. After being moved around, the club members decided they needed a permanent home and they asked Wallasey Corporation about land in Leasowe. The Council agreed to sell them their present day site in Reeds Lane in 1931. Just in front of the Rugby club, slightly to the left, is part of the old Leasowe Road. Leasowe Road was widened and straightened in 1931/32. On the other side, Leasowe Golf course and Club can be seen, also the big sandy Leasowe Bay which now no longer exists. Ahead are the market gardens of Cross, McGreal, Molloy and Freemans. Moving to the right hand side of Leasowe Road, halfway along is Gardenside, Leasowside and Meadowside. The houses were built between 1930 and 1933. Just behind the houses is the Brick works that was owned by Barker and Jones (see page 43).

The picture below shows Leasowe golf Clubs' Club House. The golf Club was formed in June 1891 on the links between Dovepoint at Meols and Lingham Lane. John Ball one of the most famous golfers of his day won the Open championship the year previously, and became the first Captain and Mr C. N. Stewart, the first Honorary Secretary. Two years later, the Club moved to its present site. (The old club became the Moreton Ladies Golf Club, see page 48, vol.1). The present Club House is the fourth on the site - one was burnt down in the 1960's and another was pulled down in the 1980's.

Both pictures on this page are of Leasowe Bay. The top one dates from the early 1920's and was taken during a storm. The little stepping stones were walked on by people, and children would hop from one stone to another. They were lost for ever when the wall was rebuilt during the 1970's.

The bottom picture dates from 1951 when regular motor bike races were run on the sand in the Bay. The sandhills can be seen in the background. The races usually occurred in August - races are occasionally run to this day. The sandhills in the picture have gone now. There is only a footpath across the top as the sand was replaced by soil and clay, and large rocks have been placed along the bottom to stop erosion.

The family picture below is of the Sutton family - their names, from left to right are - Arnold Sutton (their youngest son), mother, Lily and father, Joseph and their other son, William. The family used to run Leasoweside Farm (see facing page). It was situated behind the house on the right, half way along Leasoweside, roughly where Frobisher Road is now. The Sutton family moved away in the late 1930's after farming there for almost one hundred years. The Vyner Estate sold the land to a builder. The farm gave its name to Leasoweside. On the facing page is Leasoweside Farm. The top picture shows the front of the farm. The boy in the picture is William Sutton, the girl is the farm maid. The picture below that shows the side of the farm with the farm workers stacking the hay. It took four men all day to make one haystack. Now it takes one man with a tractor a baler only a couple of hours.

All four pictures on these pages date from 1910. The first one, at the top left, is of the Stone House which was situated in the dog-leg part of old Leasowe Road. The house was empty by the late 1930's and was pulled down soon after the war. The site is now part of Castleway Primary School's playing field.

The photographs on this page are of Liscard Farm. The farm was on the left along Gardenside, opposite Meadowside. The top picture was taken from the house on the corner of Meadowside, which was pulled down in 1961. The site is now occupied by the Catholic Church and Infants School.

The photograph below shows Mr & Mrs. Leyland who ran the farm as a market garden. The land was owned by the brickworks.

The picture on this page are of the Moreton and Leasowe brickworks. The top picture shows the brick kilns of the Leasowe Road brickworks which started in 1892, and was known as the Leasowe brickworks. They were later sold to Mr R. P.Barker and Mr T. Jones in 1900. By the 1930's it was running out of clay so they bought the Moreton brickworks in Pasture Road, near to Moreton station, which had a vast reserve of clay and was thus able to keep both kilns working. Lorries were used to transport the clay to the Leasowe Road brickworks. As many people will remember, Moreton brickworks started in 1900 and a row of houses was built called 'Sunnyside', for their workers. They also had a railway siding installed to send bricks all over the country and to Ireland. The houses in Moreton were built with Barker and Jones bricks. Just before the war, a gravel dredging machine was imported from Belgium (see below) and adapted to dig clay out. Many people will have seen these machines when walking along Lingham Lane, or when they went fishing in the old clay pits that were well-stocked with fish of all kinds. The Leasowe Road kilns closed in the late 1960's, followed by Pasture Road in the late 1970's. Mr Barker and Mr Brisco built another brickyard in Carr Lane in the 1930's; it stopped making bricks in 1992.

THE GUNPOWDER PLOT - 1831

As a happy sequel to the talk given by Mr. J. Appleyard, Dip.Ed., at our November 1963 meeting, when he spoke on 'Discovering Local History' - A school sets out to explore its environment, we are privileged to copy in print, for the first time, the Leasowe Gunpowder Mill Document. The original is written in ink in copperplate hand, on what appears to be pigskin. It was presented to Moreton C. E. School, of which Mr Appleyard was headmaster, by one of its pupils, David Griffiths, in 1961.

*   *   *   *   *   *

(William IV 1837)

To His Majesty's Justices of the Peace Assembled at the General
       Quarter Sessions of the Court (?) at nether Knutsford in the
       County of Chester.

The Memorial of the undersigned Owners of Land and Property within, and Inhabitants of the Parish of Wallasea in the same County Sheweth,

That your Memorialists have seen a notice signed by Sir John Tobin, Knight, Thomas Tobin and Thomas Tobin the junior, merchants, addressed to the churchwardens and overseers of the poor of the said Parish of Wallasea, stating the intention of applying to your worships for a licence to erect a mill or manufactory for making gunpowder and also a magazine for storing (?) gunpowder in certain places within the said Parish of Wallasea marked in a plan annexed to such notice.

That the Act of Parliament passed in the 12th Year of the reign of his late Majesty King George the 3rd (?) under the provisions of which the said Sir John Tobin and company are applying for a licence to erect the gunpowder Mill and Magazine before mentioned, prohibits any dealer in gunpowder from keeping at any one time more than two hundred pounds of gunpowder at any house or warehouse within one mile of any market town or within two miles of any existing (?) magazines or within half a mile of a Parish Church. And the same Act, after reciting that it may be necessary to have some places appointed in which it may be lawful to erect new mills for making gunpowder, gives a discretionary power to Justices in Session to licence the erection of such mills not being within the limits in the Act before particularised, as the a dealer keeping gunpowder.

That the land upon which it is proposed to erect the aforesaid mill is within five furlongs from the town of Wallasey where the Parish Church stands on an emminance, and though not a market town, contains about five hundred inhabitants and the population daily increasing: within six furlongs of Leasowe Castle; within three furlongs from the Farm House and farm buildings called Leasoweside; within one furlong and three quarters of the only public highway connecting the Parish of Wallasea with the other parts of the County of Chester; within one mile and 2-1/2 furlongs of the intended new town called New Brighton, where there are several houses and a large hotel already built and upwards of twenty streets now laid out.

That in addition to the great hazard and danger to life and property by the introductory of a manufactory of the description before mentioned in which (as is evinced at Chatham (?) and Dartford) frequent explosions and accidents occur which the utmost vigilance and watchfulness cannot prevent, your Memorialists the undersigned Land Owners will suffer a serious loss in the value of the property, in as much as the land in the Parish of Wallasea by reason of its nearness to Liverpool, and its lying upon the shore of the River Mersey and the Irish Sea, has obtained a high value as building land and several late purchases have been made at high prices with a view to the erection of villa's and residences which will be entirely stopped if a public nuisance of the nature before described is allowed to be erected.

That your Memorialist, the Honourable Sir Edward Cust has long had it in contemplation to erect at Leasowe Castle a specious hotel, sea baths, a public news room billiards rooms and several lodging houses. Plans and specifications for which are completed, and tenders for building the same have been obtained, the whole projected improvements must necessarily by abandoned if a licence should be granted to erect a gunpowder mill in the place proposed.

That your Memorialist, Robert Vyner has property adjoining to the mill fields (?) now called the Powder Mill Fields (?) and also property extending along the south side of Wallasea Pool opposite the intended magazine in the Parish of Bidston where he has expended upwards of five thousand pounds in making new and improving the roads and in giving (such access?) in the expectation —— (?) of villas and residences being erected there-on, which plans so beneficial to that part of the land (?) must be given up if a gunpowder mill is erected in the place proposed.

That the proposed magazine is intended to be erected in the district (?) within six furlongs of the mansion lately erected for the residence of your Memorialist, John Wilson, within eight furlongs of the mansion belonging to your Memorialist, James Mainwaring, with seven furlongs of the village of Poolton, in the said parish of Wallasea, within one mile and three quarters of the Seacome Town and Ferry, within one mile and five furlongs of the Egremont Ferry and Church and within one mile of Liscard Village, within one mile and six and three quarter furlongs of the present Magazines at Liscard and within four and half furlongs of Wallasey Town.

Your Memorialists therefore anxiously hope your worships will not grant a Licence for the erection of a gunpowder Mill and a Magazine in the places proposed. So dangerous to the public and so destructive of the value of private property in the neighbourhood.

R. E. Warburton	Will Jones	William Evans
by R. V. Law	Wm. Martin	Thomas Bell
R. V. Law, Rector	Lady. H. Murray	John Holyland
of Wallasey	and	Keith Hughes
J. Mainwaring of	W. C. Backhouse	Thomas Holt
Poolton Hall	by J. Mainwaring	Sarah Eaton

John Penkett
Robert Vyner and
Edward Cust
by John Davies
R Edwards
R. Smith
H. Meadows
Job Wilson
T. N. Hill
W. Peers
T. Dean
J. Davies
W. Brown
by H. Meadows
John Ball
J. A. Marsden
by I Marsden
Thos. Webster
W. Armstead
Robert Jones
Richard Jones
M. Beaconsfield
Jane Beaconsfield
Robert Carter
Thomas Mawdsley
Henry Worsley
Peggy Smith
J. D. Maddock
W. Rowson
. Atherton
by W. Rowson
N. B. Ellis
. W. Wright
., Clarke
G. Cooper
John Givon
J. Johnson
M. Hareson
by T. Pendleton
. Meadows
Leonard Craven
L. Bussard

D. Robinson
T B Hasler
I Byron
X. R. Bennet
mark for J.P.
N. Wotherston
J. Ledsham
by S. Davies
P. Ledsham
S. Harrison J.
S. Harrison S.
J. Robinson
W. Woodson
J. Dinn
J. Stanley
Ann Kemp
E. Hilton
E. Fogg
by W. Peers
J. Cartheon
W. Boome
Robert Stanley
George Nelson
Joseph William
R. Parsonage
Richard Hazler
Joseph Jones
James Dean
M. Pulforo
by S. Dean
J. Wilson
R. Parsonage
Richard Allen
R. Masne
Richard Smith and
William Mason
by S. Davies
James Pemberton
Thomas Pemberton
H. Pennant
T. Bell
R. Langton

Wm. Smith
Peter Ledder
William Lester
Harry Harris
Joseph Abram
Thomas Pemberton
John Dixon
Thomas Worthing
Allen Penswick
John Mullinen
John B. Smith
Joseph Pemberton
John Coltart
William Evans
Elizabeth Richardson
R. M. Davies
C. Jeffreys
J. Miller
Ann Green
William Stewarts
Peter Ledsham
by S. Davies
Wm. Bennett
E. Holinery
Richard Evans
John Barrow
Charles Banner
by. S. Davies
Elizabeth Ellis
Ellen Jane Dobson
James Hill
John Rimmer
Martin Scott
? by s. Davies
Richard Smith
Margaret Meadows
M. J. Foulkes
M. Rigley
Alic Hampson
by S. Davies
— Catterall

NOTES

1. Sir John Tobin lived in what is now the School of Art and had
    been connected with the slave trade.

2. No date appears on the Memorial but the following facts help — (1) Wallasey's population
    in 1831 was 558 (this seems very near); (2) Edward Cust was knighted in 1831; (3) James Ather
    ton bought 170 acres of coastline to develop at New Brighton in 1830; (4) Robert Vanburgh
    Law was Rector of Wallasey 1825 -1834.

    This indicates 1831 to 1834; as the population was rising it seems that the earlier date is most likely.

    Of the 144 signatures only one is definitely indicated by a mark

        *   *   *   *   *   *

        Note: Their miles and furlongs seem to be very elastic to say the least. The
        approximate site for the factory would be where Ross and Grant Roads (on
        the Leasowe Estate) are now. It would have given them easy access to the
        sea by using Wallasey Pool. Ships could have loaded and unloaded in
        relative safety.

        *   *   *   *   *   *

LEASOWE CASTLE

Leasowe Castle has had a long and varied history. It has gone from dereliction to resurrection on more than one occasion in its life. To tell you the story we have to back to 1593.

Leasowe Castle was built in 1593 by Ferdinando, the 5th Earl of Derby. The original building, which is still standing, is an octagonal tower, four storeys high, and has a carved date stone bearing the date 1593 above the three Legs of Man the Derby's were the Lords of Man. The castle was known as 'New Hall' until 1802. It has been said it was used as a 'view-point' to watch the Wallasey Races but this is unlikely with the finishing line over two miles away, this seems implausible.

It was most likely used for hunting and falconing and the most likely of all was that it was a 'safe place; to come and go the Isle of Man and Ireland, with the Horse Channel on its doorstep. As there were turbulent times, the tower was later enlarged, some time between 1600 and 1642, with four square towers built on alternate faces of the tower. It was about this time that horse racing began on the Leasowes (meaning Meadowes). It was a straight course between the Castle and approximately the bottom of Sandiways Road, the stables being at the top.

The first mention of racing at Leasowe was by a man called Webb, in 1608. It was probably the earliest establishment of horse racing in the country - it was a straight course as previously mentioned.

By 1723, it was decided by Lord Derby, Sir Richard Grosvenor, Mr. Egerton and eight others, to pay twenty guineas per annum for ten years, to be raced for on the Wallasey course on the first Thursday in May. It was the richest race in the country and quickly outgrew its remote site. The Wallasey Stakes as it became known moved to Newmarket and then to Epsom. It was still being run on the first Thursday in May until 1790. Although it is open to argument, it does appear to have evolved into the classic three year olds race 'The Derby'.

The 'Derby's' always chose the wrong side and lost their heads. James, the 7th Earl, lost his head in 1651, in Bolton. The Castle became rundown and got the name 'Mockbeggar Hall' (Mockbeggar meaning 'to mock a beggar unfit to live in'. By 1682 it was lived in again and racing began again with James, Duke of Monmouth, winning the race on his own horse. By the end of the seventeenth century, it was used as a farmhouse until 1770, when it came into the possession of the Egerton's of Oulton through Chancery. They lived in it until Mr Egerton's death in 1778. The Castle stayed empty for eight years and was then bought by Mr Robert Harrison, who in turn sold it after sixteen years, in 1802 to the widow of Lewis Boode, a West Indian Planter. It was at this transaction that the name changed from 'New Hall' to Leasowe Castle, with the Bill of Sale calling it thus. It certainly sounded greater than 'New Hall' did. Mrs Boode made many alterations to the building and gardens, and she also allowed her home to be used as a hospital by the survivors of the many shipwrecks that used to occur on this part of the coast. Mrs Boode died on April 21st 1926 when she went out for a drive in her carriage. She fell out of the carriage and struck her head on a rock on the road. It happened on Breck Road, Wallasey just where the bridge is that crosses the tunnel approach road.

There is a monument to commemorate the incident that reads thus:

"Near this spot, Mrs Boode of Leasowe Castle, was killed by a fall from her pony carriage - April XXI MDCCCXXVI. May ye who pass by respect this memorial of an awful dispensation and the affectionate tribute of any only child to perpetuate her dear mother's memory beyond the existence of that breast which will never cease to cherish it. Ah! may the sad remembrance which attaches to this spot, impress on every one this salutary warning - 'In the midst of life we are in death'."

Leasowe Castle was inherited by her only child, a daughter, Mary Anne, who married Sir Edward Cust K.C.B. (the sixth son of the First Lord Brownlow of Belton, Lincolnshire. In 1821, Sir Edward Cust and the Cust family have had a long association with royalty. Sir Edward was Master of Ceremonies to the Queen until 1876. He was knighted in the early 1830's. In May 1828, Col. Cust turned Leasowe Castle into an hotel. This was not a great success so he closed it down and used it as his country seat. He made a lot of improvements whilst there. On the demolition of the old Exchequer Buildings, Whitehall, in 1836 (which with the Houses of Parliament were destroyed by fire in 1832) he bought the original panelling from the Star Chamber and also parts of the ceiling and fireplaces from the same room. It was called the Star Chamber and was used as a dining room. The library was panelled in the dark bog oak taken from the submerged forest that went from Leasowe to Meols. The surrounding wall with the Gate House and the main gate were also built by him at the same time.

Sir Edward was made a baronet on his retirement from Master of Ceremonies to the Queen. He died on January 14th 1878, aged 83. He achieved great literary distinction for his work in nine volumes of the Annals of the Wars of the 18th and 19th centuries, and other books on the same subjects. The Castle continued to be inhabited by the Dowager Lady Cust. The Castle was put up for sale by auction on June 17th 1893 but was withdrawn. It was again put up for auction in September 1895. It was sold for £9,500 and was opened soon after as the Leasowe Castle Hotel. It was a minor success but was again put up for auction on the 14th August, 1908 but failed to reach its reserve price of £11,500. It was eventually sold with all its contents to the Trustees of the Railway Convalescent Homes in 1910. The Trustees spent £2,500 on various alterations. It was only the second home they had, the first being in Herne Bay. It was known as the King Edward VII Memorial Convalescent Home for Railwaymen (to give it its full title) but very quickly shortened to the Railway Convalescent Home. It was taken over for the duration of the first World War from August 5th 1914 to 1918. It held several hundred German prisoners of war from August 17th 1917 until the end of the war. It was then given back to the Trustees in early 1919. It was originally for railwaymen but later in the 1930's, it changed and became women only. It finally closed in ? 1969 and was bought by Wallasey Council, who did not know what to do with it and eventually sold it to Mr Ken Harding for £50,000 and he turned it into an hotel once more.

Another date that will be recalled in the future when people look back, will be September 9th, 1992, when it caught fire in the early afternoon. Workmen were carrying our safety work on the upper floors and in the roof space. Fortunately, the wind was coming from the West and not off the sea, otherwise the damage would have been far worse, if not fatal. It has cost £1,250,000 to be repaired.

The top picture shows the Castle as it would have looked in 1593. The pictures below date from 1870 and shows Lord and Lady Cust.

The top picture is of the Cust family coach and driver and dates from 1880. The picture below dates from 1900 and shows Sir Charles Cust in the back seat, wearing a black hat. He is equerry to the Duke of York (later King George V). The driver is the Hon. C. S. Rolls and he is with his father, Lord Llangattock, who is sitting on the back seat wearing a light coloured hat. The car is a 12 h.p. Panhard.

Above is the main gate and Gatehouse in 1900. Below is the Gatekeeper's Lodge and the Mermaid Stones. the main gate to the shore is just around the corner. the remains of a "pillbox" is on the site now.

Both pictures date from the early 1900's. The top one shows it as an hotel and below the main entrance hall and stairs.

B 3752. LEASOWE CASTLE, ENTRANCE HALL.

The top picture dates from 1911 when some alterations were being made to the Convelescent Home to be. Below is the Star Chamber dating from the 1910's.

Both pictures date from 1911. The top one was taken on 12th June, 1911 and shows the Mayoress of Liverpool, Mrs Mason Hutchinson, being presented with the key, after opening the Home, with the help of the Mayor and Mayoress of Wallasey. Below shows one of the first postcards with the full title, which was soon shortened to the Railway Convalescent Home.

LEASOWE CASTLE NOW

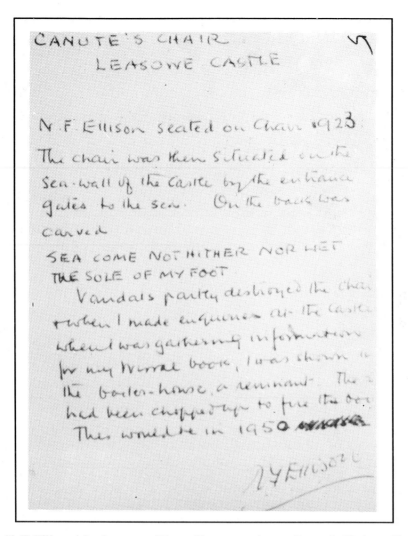

CANUTE'S CHAIR
LEASOWE CASTLE

N. F. Ellison seated on chair 1923.
The chair was then situated on the
sea-wall of the castle by the entrance
gates to the sea. On the back was
carved

SEA COME NOT HITHER NOR WET
THE SOLE OF MY FOOT
    Vandals partly destroyed the chair
+ when I made enquiries at the castle
when I was gathering information
for my Wirral book, I was shown in
the boiler-house, a remnant. The ?
had been chopped up to feed its fire.
    This would be in 1950

Above is a letter from Mr. N. F. Ellison (also known as 'Nomad') commenting on Canute's Chair, and below sitting on the Chair in 1923.

Above - the Castle shortly after Mr Harding took it over and opened it as an hotel again. Below, dating 9th September, 1992, when a fire broke out in the roof.

Above - the day after (10th September, 1992). The firemen were still damping down.

Below - (10th January, 1993) showing tysons, the building firm doing the repair work.

LEASOWE HOSPITAL

The Leasowe Sanatorium for Crippled Children and Hospital for Surgical Tuberculosis, to give its full and original name, later became known as the Liverpool Open-Air Hospital, Leasowe, and finally as the heading states.

To write a short history or anything at all about the hospital, one name above all others stands out and that is Margaret Beavan (born 1877, died 1931). She was the driving force, admired by all, she was known affectionately as the Little Mother of Liverpool, also not quite as complimentary - the 'Mighty Atom' and 'Clever Beggar'. Even at school, she did not like to lose and though only small, she entered all sports with great determination. She later became Head Girl and even at this early age she was endeavouring to help the poor in some small way. Her first effort was to cajole the other girls to join her in giving a Christmas tree to the poor of the dockland. She eventually went on to Liverpool University. Whilst there, she joined the Kyrle Society, who were philanthropists, who gave money out of their own pockets to help the poor. Upon leaving University, she rented a small room in the middle of the slums, as an office. During this time she came to the notice of a Mr A V Paton (he was later knighted), who was a remarkable man who devoted just about all of his time to helping children and the West Kirby Convalescent Home for Children (the first of its kind in the country).

With his guidance, they started in 1891 the Invalid Children's Aid. It was built around a London model founded a few years earlier. It was manned by volunteers who tried to help sick children to go to the country for convalescent. It was a haphazard and disorganised affair. They literally picked children up off the streets. It was starting to get beyond the means of the Kyrle Society, so they had to look for help somewhere else, and in due course, they joined with the Crippled Childrens' Workshops that was doing well. This led to a name changing and a new start. So in the January of 1908, the Invalid Children's Association was founded. The name was to change once again when in 1919 it became the Liverpool Child Welfare Association. Margaret Beavan was its chief from its inception in 1907 until her death ion 1931. The Association's work covered a large area, although it started in Liverpool, its work stretched from Runcorn to Ellesmere Port to Bootle and Birkenhead, and the surrounding areas. By the 1970's, all its work had been taken over by the National Health Service and the Department of Health and Social Security. The Association still exists but only as a legal entity. It still owns its premises in Copperas Hill which was rented to the Woman's Royal Volunteers Service, but is now closed.

Margaret Beavan became the first woman Lord Mayor of Liverpool in 1927/28. She also officiated at the break-through of the first Mersey Tunnel (the Queensway) in 1931. She caught a cold and developed pneumonia and died. She was also a Magistrate and spent all her life as a volunteer worker.

The first mention of a Sanatorium for T.B. children occurred on the 16th December, 1911. At a Committee Meeting, after communication with the Medical Officer of Health and the Education Committee, it appeared that they were to receive a grant of up to 3/5th's of the capital cost. The next meeting held on 23rd January, 1912, Sir G. Newman of the Whithall Board of Education, indicated that as far as he could see from the plans submitted, the Sanatorium would get approval from the Board; and as regards to capital expenditure, it would be prepared to make a grant of £70 - £90 per bed and 50% of the maintenance costs for all children sent by the Municipal. By this time, a site had been found in Leasowe. The Board of Education sent a number of staff down the next day to inspect the site.

At another meeting on the 13th February, 1913, it was confirmed that the site was acceptable. The deeds were drawn up and the Association was incorporated. Everything was set in motion - an appeal was sent out to over 5,000 people in Liverpool with regard to the Leasowe Sanatorium; a parliamentary list of donations had already reached £6,731; there were four sums of £1,000 donated by George Holt, Miss Holt of Holt Shipping Lines, Mr H Harrison of The Harrison Shipping Lines and Mr A V Paton in memory of his wife. Further donations from the Brocklebank family were received also many others soon swelled the coffers.

The next step was to purchase the land and this happened on the 17th April, 1913. The land was owned by the Webster family and farmed by the Beed family.

Under the heading **Transactions with regard to Leasowe**: it was reported that the contract had already been signed, that the estate had been purchased - part of the money having been paid on signing, the balance to be completed when the Association's possession of the said property on September 1st, 1913 - the price being £3,600, 17th April, 1913.

They also tried to buy the land opposite the hospital on the shore side, now used for car boot sales, from a Mr. Sparks who wanted more than they could afford.

The Association agreed to renew the tenancy of these fields with Mr. Beed for three months, at the same rental he had paid before, namely £10 per annum. By the 14th August, 1913, the Committee had asked and received tenders from ten building firms, listed below:-

Names of Contractors	Units a: b:	Units c:	Totals
Messrs. W. Thornton	£3,115	£4,056	£7,171
" W. Hall & Sons	£3,055	£3,975	£7,030
" Joshua Henshaw	£3,967	£3,860	£6,827
" Tomkinson & Co	£2,900	£3,800	£6,700
" J & G Chappel	£2,745	£3,612	£6,357
" Morrison & Son	£2,610	£3,460	£6,070
" Jones & Sons £2,580	£3,420	£3,420	£6,000
" W. H. Forde & Sons	£2,490	£3,370	£5,861
" James Merritt £2,489	£3,346	£5,835	£5,385
" Brown & Backhouse	£2,500	£3,230	£5,730

The Sub Committee asked the Council to empower them to negotiate with Messrs Brown & Backhouse since theirs was the lowest tender.

An Executive Committee meeting was held the next day - 14th August, 1913. The Secretary reported that the tender by Messrs. Brown & Backhouse had formally been accepted, namely £2,500 for Blocks A & B, and £3,230 for Block C - in total £5,730. Messrs Brown & Backhouse had already commenced work on the 11th August, 1914. The work was completed on time and the first children were taken into Faith Block on 7th July, 1914. The Commemorative Stone was laid on 21st July, 1914. The total cost of building the hospital was £180,000.

The first years running cost in 1947 (before the National Health Service took over) was £47,844. 2s.0d. There was no effective cure for tuberculosis until the 1940's when a Ukrainian scientist, Selman Waksman, working in the U.S.A., discovered the drug Streptomycin. It was an antibiotic and stopped the tubercle bacillus from multiplying. Slowly Leasowe Hospital changed from being principally a children's T. B. hospital to one for dealing with burns and skin grafts, and then arthritis until its closure in 1979. It was bought by the Wirral Christian Centre in 1981 and is now used as a Retirement Home and Handicap Centre, and many other activities as well.

The picture below shows the hospital in 1935, notice the gas lamps.

The picture above is of Miss Margaret Beavan taken in the late 1910's. Below is the Liverpool Child Welfare Centre in Copperas Hill. It started life as the Invalid Children's Association in 1908 and closed down in 1970's, by then it was known as the Child Welfare Centre. It was then rented out to the W.R.V.S. until the 1980's. The premises are now unoccupied but my personal opinion is that I feel it should be opened as a museum to let people see how things were, and also to honour Miss Margaret Beavan, and all the other people who assisted her, for without them, it would not have been possible.

The above picture dates from 1909. The white cottages and the grey building (once known as Leasowe Hotel and later the Webster's family home), until it was sold to build the hospital. In the background of the picture, shows where the hospital was built. The grey building became the Nurses Home until it was pulled down in 1923, due to dampness. Below is an aerial photograph of the hospital taken in 1920. The bricks and timber from the Nurses Home were cleaned and used to build four bungalows in Ditton Lane to house the 'maintenance staff' at a cost of £950. The bungalows were finished in October 1923.

Above shows the Laying of the Foundation Stone by Lord Derby on the 21st July, 1914. Although it reads 'the Countess of Derby' on the stone, her ladyship was indisposed. Lord Derby is the man standing behind the man bending down. The man on the extreme right of the picture is Mr. T. W. Haig, the architect. The lady in the middle with the bouquet of flowers, is Miss Margaret Beavan. Also present is the Mayor of Liverpool and many dignitaries of the day. The picture below, taken in 1917, was when Queen Mary visited the hospital. It was a private arrangement by Margaret Beavan as King George was visiting Birkenhead. To the right of Queen Mary is the Matron, Miss Charlotte Hughes, and to the left is Margaret Beavan. The sole man in the picture is Mr T. W. Haig. The first patients had arrived two weeks earlier, when four children were carried into Faith ward on the 7th July, 1914.

The top picture shows the Lord mayor of Liverpool on a visit to the hospital. On the right of the picture, the Matron, Miss E. M. Tucker (who incidentally was the first Matron) is just to his left , Margaret Beavan is in the middle, and other dignitaries on a visit. Below shows another Lord Mayor and Mayoress on a visit.

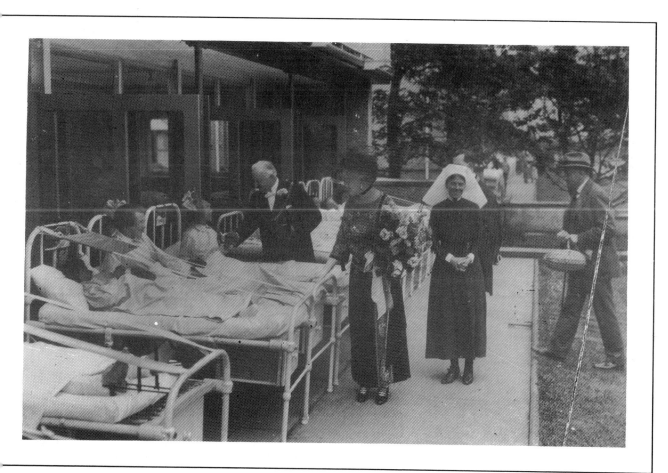

Above is a picture taken in 1914, of some of the first arrival for the hospital, arriving at Leasowe station. There was no transport in the first year so everyone was either carried, pushed or pulled to the hospital, over what was just a 'dirt track'. It remained thus until 1930/31 when the road was made fit for traffic.

The picture below shows the Nurses' Rest Room. It was situated on the fromnt of the building (facing the railway with its back to the sea), overlooking Honour Ward but gave a good view of the gardens.

Above shows Hope Ward (Block) just after it was opened in 1914. Below is Faith Ward (Block) in 1917, part of it being used as a Baby Ward. Originally all the main buildings were known as 'Blocks'. Each Block was split into four wards and each Block had a name - Loyalty, Honour, Faith, Hope and Observation, and later Sunlight was added. 'Honour' was split up into five wards, all with names as follows- Heath Harrison, Violet, A.P. Paton, Edith Davell and Herbert Bickersteth Wards. Most, if not all the beds, were named after people who donated enough money to cover the cost of a bed.

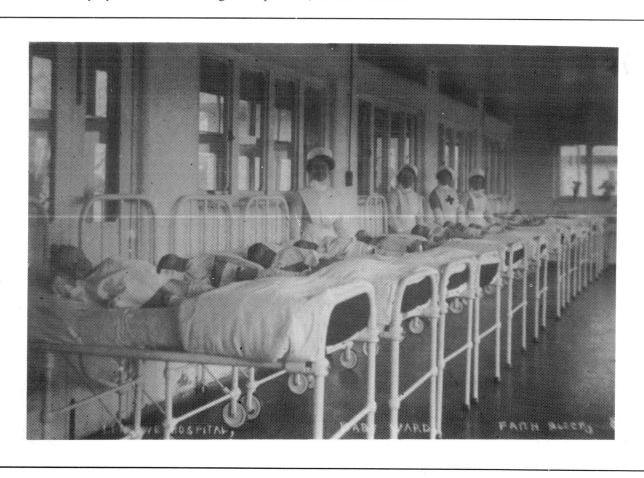

Both pictures were taken at Christmastime in 1922. The top picture shows the adult female patients who were in Loyalty ward. The rest of the wards were divided between girls, boys and babies. The picture below shows Father Christmas calling on Faith Ward with his presents. Faith Ward was divided between babies and boys. The money to buy the presents was raised by having large 'sales of goods' that were donated by shops and people. St. George's Hall was one of the places where these 'sales' were held.

As can be seen in the top picture, there were no computers in those days - everything was done by hand. After just five years, they had dealt with 55,000 cases. Below shows 'Dick Kerr's Ladies' Football team. They used to play charity matches, mainly in the North West. They used to attract large crowds and occasionally represent England in international matches against a French ladies team. The did a lot to swell the coffers of a lot of charities. Dick Kerr ran an Engineering firm in Preston. The British Aerospace occupied the site and the original buildings.

There used to be several Open Days each year when donors could come and see how their money was used. During the summer, trips out were arranged and many people came in their private cars to take the children for a ride. Also, local coach firms would lend a coach and driver as in the picture above taken about 1920.

Below from left to right are:- The Alderman, Deputy Lord Mayor of Liverpool, G. Whitehead, Mayor of Bury; Vicary Scoins, Mayor of Wallasey; Edward Burrows, Mayor of St. Helens; James O'Neill, Mayor of Bootle; Charles McVoy, Mayor of Birkenhead; T. Halsted, Mayor of Bolton. Again this was a special day arranged for the Mayors to visit to see how they could help; as children were sent from all over the country, but mainly from the North West. This picture was taken in 1946 - one of the last of its type as the National Health Service took over in 1948.

It did not matter what the weather was like, as can be seen in the top picture taken in the winter of 1934/35 when snow was lying on the ground. Good food, sunshine and plenty of fresh air was the remedy. All the children wore red woollen hats and mittens.

Below shows the back of the building - as the front faced south to catch the sun. this picture was taken in the 1930's.

LEASOWE CHILDRENS HOSPITAL AND COMMON.   No 3321

TWENTY MORE QUESTIONS
IN AND ABOUT MORETON

1. When Moreton was yet a rural village
    Devoted to dairying, haymaking and tillage.
    Where the dunes by Arrowe Brook sprawl.
    What there was shared by local farmers all

    Relics of feudalism, largely green fallows,
    They were the ancient Moreton Town Meadows.

2. Between the First and Second Wars strife
    What local Club led a nomadic life
    Roslyn Drive, clap Lane and The Carr, but a few
    Of the sites this Club once very well knew.

    Not until the fifties did it attain permanency
    The club is the redoubtable Moreton A.F.C.

3. During postwars depressed and doleful days
    On a site off Sandbrook where cattle did graze
    What event starred the sporting world's best
    "Dixie", Donoghue, Tarleton and the rest

    From Wirral over Woodside to West Kirby
    They came to support Moreton Donkey Derby.

4. What once had life in a wooden army hut
    Which when erected by Christchurch was put
    Service veterans returned from war
    For these it had ever a welcoming door

    Today prefixed Royal, the pride of our region
    It is - yes Sir, Moreton Royal British Legion.

5. What name was given to the Railwayside pond
    Of which local anglers were extremely fond
    Excavated for clay to give the road elevation
    Where the Line crosses at Moreton station

    Named after the man who filled Foreman's role
    it was the once celebrated Black Harry's Hole.

6. What once stood on the Hoylake Road site
    presently suffered from demolition blight
    It awaits development for a new erection
    A superstore, I think, but I'm open to correction

    There it was I learned the Three R's Rule
    It was of course, Moreton original school.

7. What once was the name of the plot of land
    Which occupies Barnston Lane's bottom left hand
    Today used for scholarly pursuits
    In a nearby pub the name had its roots

    From older locals, the answers not concealed
    They knew it well as Billy Hale's Field. ·

8. Presently a hospital overlooking the Shore
    Who built it and why, in old days of yore
    They also raised structures on a much higher perch
    The Manor House, Upton and the Mansion, Overchurch

    Like these it was built as a family residence
    But the name Webster gives the answer sense.

9. For a century or more, through every season and clime
    What reminded scholars to heed well the time
    Most mornings and noons throughout the year
    Intoning brief message, both lucid and clear

    Brave was the scholar who ignored its knell
    It was the loud clanger - Moreton School Bell.

10. A brand new invention, with strange sounding name
    What was the vehicle which in the fifties came
    An experimental service, to test its true score
    It plied between Moreton and Rhyl's distant shore

    With plastic skirt and aerial propellers aft
    Clearly it was - the original Hovercraft

11. What planned as a pub thanks to legal nonsense
    Was point-blank refused a public licence
    Converted to a residence, and sometime Cafe
    It yet is upstanding to this very day

    Pasture Roads last house, the Common it overlooks
    Name it Castle Blake, to get off my hooks.

12. What pub had a garden at its rear
    Where folk could eat, sup wine and swill beer
    Snugged on a lawn neath shady pear trees
    It was a suntrap entirely screened from the breeze

    If stumped, please don't ask any pardon
    Only older folk know Farmers Arms had a
    garden.

13. What Moreton thoroughfare is of singular fame
    No other in the village can boast of this same
    Even through Wallasey's name changing spate
    It has managed to retain its peculiar state

    To answer this riddle requires no great feat
    The thoroughfare is Chadwick - Moreton's only street.

14. What Moreton pub has a religious connotation
    Not Coach & Horses, I hasten to mention
    No - this pub's situated farther from the Cross
    The late Joe Wharton was one time it's boss.

    It then bore a sign depicting equine charms
    And a caption reading - Plough Inn Druids Arms

15. What Moreton team, of the twenties soccer scene
    Had a centre forward - the great "Dixie Dean"
    This was, of course, at the start of his fame
    Before he was payed for playing the game

    Even then he could net any pass
    For the very junior - Moreton Bible Class

16. What on the Common stood round the last bend
    Just at the left of Lingham Lane's end
    Built as a Pavilion - this edifice was founded
    For a venture which failed and sadly was grounded

    Any old Moretonian with wit, sense and nous
    Will instantly remember the old Golf House.

17.   What Moreton jockey, I'll give you three guesses
   Built shops and named them after his successes
   This pointer I'll add, then you'll understand
   The Grand national he won on famous "Kirkland"

   Drink now a toast to the revered memory
   Of jockey "Tich" mason, for surely it was he

18.   In post first war Moreton, entirely unlit
   Side roads were boggy, for night travel unfit
   Because night wayfarers had lanterns to hand
   What nearby district was dubbed Fairyland

   The answer to kill any lingering doubt
   Is - overchurch Road and environs about

19.   Snugged in the shade of a small Oak wood
   Before the Co-op what on that site stood
   It had white-washed walls (I've photographic proof)
   But most picturesque was its olde-worlde roof

   Dating before infamous Guy Fawkes Plot age
   It was indeed an old thatched cottage

20.   When the motor superseded horse and landau
   What name had the bus which shoreward did go
   Rough, bumpy roads made each journey a fright
   Yet it plied until a late hour each night

   In giving you the answer, I'll tell you true
   It was Tom Mason's celebrated "Cuckoo".

Floods in Moreton now occur mainly in people's back gardens after a heavy downpour and on the fields in Fender Lane where it is still prone to water-logging. In the wet autumn of 1992, there was water everywhere and it looked like one big lake for months. the original problem areas were at leasowe, Moreton Shore and Lingham, but have now more or less been overcome due to the widening and clearing of the rivers - Birket, Arrowebrook and Fender on a regular basis, and the installation of automatic pumps at the end of the culvert that all these rivers run into. The culvert then runs underground by Birkenhead North station, and then down to Morpeth Dock, where the pumps come on when the water reaches a certain level.

The pictures on these pages, starting with the one above, dates from the spring of 1906. It is opposite the lighthouse. The picture below was taken about 1924 in Town Meadow where Curlew Way, Tern Way, Wastdale Drive and Mallard Way are now. the four men in the picture are Mr. Glover, Mr Bernard, Mr Smith and Mr Faves. They are carrying an elderly lady who is not well, to safety from her flooded home.

The picture above is showing children walking in the flood water on Pasture Road by the River Birket - it dates from 1927. The barn in the background was part of Pasture Farm which has now been moved to the top of Pasture Road.

The picture below left, was taken in 1927 also but in Reeds Lane (by Reedville Grove). The bus in the picture is a Crosville.

The Crosville Company was the first bus company to run a bus services into or through Moreton. The first service to run in Moreton was run by Mr. Coles of Birkenhead (see page 87, Vol. 1). The picture below, on the right, was taken in 1938 opposite to where the Catholic Church is now. It was one of two places notorious for flooding at Moreton Cross - the other being in Pasture Road where the zebra crossing is now. The first bus in the picture, is a Birkenhead bus, the second is a Wallasey bus.

More pictures of floods. This time in Ditton lane in November 1944. The two bungalows in the top picture belonged to the hospital. The picture below is also of Ditton Lane looking towards Reeds Lane The nearest bungalow has been pulled down and abrick one built in its place. The white bungalow, behind the new bungalow, was built in the early 1920's. It is still standing and owned by the Murray family. The next bungalow is still standing, but the others have been replaced by brick ones.

This picture is of Leasowe Tennis Club. It was founded in the early 1920's and finally closed in the middle 1970's. The Club was situated between Reedville Grove and Leasowe station. The top picture is of Mrs. J. E. Davies above 'to serve'. The Club House can be seen on the left-hand side of the picture. The members played for a 'Rose Bowl' every year; below shows a group of members outside the Club House - the picture dating from the 1930's. It was owned and run by the Hart family.

Sunfield Road in 1927. It stretched from the bottom of Danger Lane to Leasowe Station.

The top picture is photographed looking towards Leasowe Station. The shops on the left had their backs to the railway. These buildings were later pulled down in the early 1930's after being condemned by the Wallasey council. Most of the people then bought marquee tents and went back to camping. In the wintertime, they would store their tents at the Bostock's farm that was half way along Danger Lane, on the right hand side, about where the houses are between Eastway and Blundells Drive. After the war, the council built the rest of Pasture Avenue and then Sunfield Road, on the old camping site.

The picture below shows the Bungalow Cafe in 1922. It was by Leasowe Station where the car park is now, but was pulled down in the mid 1930's. The names of the two gentlemen in the picture are Mr. Simpson on the left and Mr. Taberner on the right.

Kingsmead Field started in the early 1910's. It started with tents and then quickly changed to something more permanent during the 1920's, as can be seen in the top left hand picture. The top right hand picture shows the ditch that was used as an open sewer and a dumping place for tins and bottles. These buildings were also condemed in the 1920's. Again people went back to using marquee tents until the Second World War. By the mid to late 1930's, they had begun to build houses to live in as can be seen in the picture below. The new road was called Kingsmead Road after the field's name. The field was owned and run by Mr. J. Cole.

Avondale park began in the early 1910's and was owned by the Osborne family, and like the other camping fields mentioned, ran from Reeds Lane to Danger Lane where Daneswell Drive, the Catholic School built in 1934, and Avondale Road are now. It was a large and well-maintained site with over 75 caravans, and a large playing and games area in the middle. The land for the St. Thomas A'Becket Catholic School was donated by the Osborne family. The park gave its name to Avondale Road.

The picture, bottom left, dates from the early days when most of the people used bell tents. They can just be seen on the right of the picture. Some of the wooden dwellings were no larger than a garden shed, as can be seen by the bottom picture. Things had improved a lot 15 or so years later; not a tent to be seen and the majority of the summer homes were of a reasonable size. They were not to be there much longer, for by 1930 they had all been condemned and pulled down. Unlike some of the other sites that had tents on them until the late 1930's. Houses and a school were being built on this site, so by 1940 most of the old site was pulled down. Between Avondale and Kingsmead Park, where Saxon Road is now, were the fellowship Fields No.s 8 & 9.

Avondale Park Camping Ground, Leasowe.

In the picture below taken in 1924, you can see Fellowship Stores on the extreme left, this was Field No. 8. It was run by Mr & Mrs Miles from 1920 until it was condemned and pulled down in 1934. The building in the middle of the picture was their home, and like many people of that period, they built it themselves. It was built in Kelly's Wood Yard by Mr. Miles and then a team of horses pulled it to its site on fellowship Field No. 8.

The picture above shows Fender Lane in 1953 before it became a dual carriageway.

The picture below dates from the early 1920's. Saxon Road and the plot of land on Reeds Lane now occupy what was Pickles Field. They were pulled down in the early 1930's. In the background of the picture can be seen the roof of the the big house that still stands in Reeds Lane - it was known as The Big House. The bungalow just to the right of the house, the roofs can just be seen, were condemed and pulled down in the late 1960's.

The top icture is of Armchair Cottage and the bottom one of Armchair Farm . They got their names from two large chairs that were cut in-to shape in hedges. One was on the left, see top picture and one was on the right of the bottom picture. The farm was run by Mr George Smith for 57 years, until it was bought by the Wallasey Council and was condemned and pulled down in 1947. The farm consisted of six acres and was run as a small holding with pigs, cows, hens and vegetables. The house opposite the Armchair pub are now on the site of the farm and the school playing fields oppposite the shops was the site of Armchair Cottage all so known as Clyde Cottage. Both pictures date from the 1910's.

The Moreton Engineering Company was founded in 1934 and the original four directors were Mr. Griffiths, Mr. A. W. Fletcher, Mr. Bradley and Dr. Clark, later Mr George Munday became Works Director. The Company was bought out by Chadburn (a Bolton engineering company) in 1976 and was moved to Bolton, the name was dropped at the same time. The company was well known worldwide. The Moreton Glasswasher was used in most public houses and clubs, and they also supplied the Royal Navy and most cruise ships. They were among the first company's to advertise on television when ITV started. Their advertisements were shown on Sunday afternoons and also in most of the national Sunday papers. The Washer was the only one of its type in the world. During the Second World War the company made parts for tanks. Both pictures were taken in the late 1950's. The buildings on the extreme left of the top picture have been pulled down and is the car park for A.T.S. (the Car Tyre and Exhaust Co). They were the original buildings used by Mr. Thom, the printer. The rest of the building was built in three stages. The last one, as can be seen in the top picture, with the change of colour in the brick was the extension upwards in the mid 1950's, to supply more office space.

The picture below shows the inside of the building and the production line. The names of the staff, from left to right, are: Arthur Pulson, Bob McKinnon, Joe Cheadle (sitting), Johnny Fell, Harry Cunliffe and George Munday.

The picture at the top is of Chapelhill Road taken in 1927. The first bungalow on the left is just before Carnsdale Road. There are now several detached houses and bungalows on the right. Just beyond the white asbestos bungalow is a line of semi's to the corner of Carnsdale Road.

The picture below shows Chapelhill Stores. It was built in 1920 by Jack Lampkin, who later sold it to the Fleming family. It finally closed its doors in 1985 - the Roberts family owning it at that time. The lady in front of the shop is Mrs. Mary Lampkin. The Lampkin family were one of Moreton's many Coal Merchants - by 1986 they were the only Coal Merchants left in Moreton. Later in that year they finally stopped delivering, thus becoming, after 66 years, by far the oldest and also the last. The family now do only haulage.

The top picture is of Sandbrook Lane taken about 1905. the postman in the picture is Jack Rutledge. The wall just on his left is where the big house called 'Davonport House' is now, and is now No. 26.

Below is Pinetree Grove, looking down Chapelhill Road. As can be seen by this road and many others, Cheshire County Council would not do anything about the roads, despite the well built homes. When the Wallasey Council took Moreton over, the first thing they did was to make good roads, but still the name 'Moreton in the Mud' has been hard to shake off. Even now, when people see pictures like these, it is partly understandable. The Dodd family lived in the top bungalow and the Francis family in the third bungalow down.

The first picture is of Carnsdale Road (then Durban Road) taken in the mid 1920's, looking towards Sandbrook Lane. The third building up, on the left, was used as a Gospel Hall until it was pulled down several years later.

The picture below is of Sandbrook Lane in 1930 and was to stay like this until the early 1960's. The bungalows on the right are still standing. The one with the roof just showing is where Holmside Close is now. It all soon changed when the builders, Mr. Whitmore and tommy Wallace started to build Grampian Way and all the other roads in that area.

Lomond Grove in 1951. The bungalow on the extreme left is still standing. It was a chicken farm once and was run by Mr. Taylor.

Below is Hoylake Road in 1953. The Council houses on the left have not long been built and on the right hand side you can see the newsagents shop that was known as Mannings and is still their on the corner of Chapelhill Road being run by Mr & Mrs. Timperley. The houses on that side were built in the 1960's by Boyd's, the builders.

Hawthorne Road, now Orchard Road, was built in the late 1890,s. All the houses in the picture are still there.

Below shows Hoylake Road which was also known as Main Road at that time, in the early 1910's. On the left of the picture is the gate to the Presbyterian Church, with the oil lamp on the arch over the entrance. The cyclist in the middle of the road certainly could not ride along the middle of any road now.

Brooklands Farm above, picture taken about 1910, was owned by the Timmis family who came from Liverpool and had a fruit import business. They used this house as their summer home until the 1900's. It had seven bedrooms upstairs and four large rooms downstairs, also a large kitchen. the tenant was Mr. Jeffrey from 1895 to 1915. In 1915 he married Miss Wilson of Hawthorne Cottage across the road, and moved over there to live. He then let the lease on the farm go to Mr. Francis of New Brighton, who ran a Laundry called the 'Sweet Lavender Laundry'. He stayed there for three or four years. Then Mr. Smith took it over just after the war until the 1950's, when the land was bought by the Catholic Church. With Brooklands Farm having so many rooms, the various tenants took in lodgers and holidaymakers in the summer months. The lady in the picture is Mrs Bradley who used to come very year for a week's holiday at Whitsun-time.

Below is a picture of Moreton Cross, looking towards Birkenhead. The shop on the right was the Post Office run by Mr. J. Dean (it is the Pet Shop now), the Post office later moved to where the Leeds Building Society is now, next to Johnson's the Cleaners, on the other side of the Cross. Just to the left of the Post Office can be seen Smith's Farm (Brooklands) and Stanley's Farm which is the light coloured one on the corner of Sandbrook Lane. This part of the road opposite the farm used to suffer from heavy flooding (see page 62 Vol. 1 and in this book on page 77) until the 1960's when the drainage was improved with the building of the Grampian Way Estate.

The cottage in both these pictures was a well-known landmark until the mid 1950's, when it was pulled down. The name of the cottage was 'The Hawthornes' after the two hawthorn trees in the garden (as seen in the middle of the top picture). The cottage was also known as Wilson's or Jeffrey's Cottage. Miss Wilson married Mr John Jeffrey who was the tenant of 'Brooklands'. The Wilsons had been tenants from 1850 to 1955 and they rented it from the Vyner family. Motor World, (the car accessory shop and garage), that was built next to Poston's Garage, is on the site now. Of all the changes that have occurred in Moreton, this one is still talked about with sadness at it being pulled down. The lady on the left of the top picture is Mrs. Phillips, her husband was the licensee of the Plough Inn, that was on the left of the cottage. The lady in the doorway of the cottage below is Mrs. Wilson, Mrs. Jeffrey's mother. Both pictures date from the middle 1890's.

The Presbyterian Church is the second oldest church in Moreton, the first being the Parish Church in Upton Road. It began in 1905 after the Hoylake Presbyterian Church had started a mission to Moreton in the summer of that year. There was a growing population and a large holiday community to cater for. There was no non-conformist church in Moreton at that time so it filled a large gap for the local people and the holiday makers who needed to go to church. The first service was held in the upper room of the Assembly Rooms which stood at the rear of the old Plough Inn. The service was held by the Rev. J. Calvin Thomas who was ably assisted by Lay preachers. It quickly became very popular and it was decided to build a chapel, so a fund was started. Enough money was soon raised and the land was bought on the corner of Knutsford Road/Hoylake Road. The Memorial Stones were laid on the 7th February, 1906. The chapel was completed and duly opened on the 15th June, 1906 by Mrs. W. T. Lever (later Lady Lever) who was presented with the key, the gift of Mr. R. Roberts, J. P.

The first service was held from 3.00 - 3.30pm. There was also a special evening service and all those going to this service were invited to the home of Mr. & Mrs. Griffiths at 'The Grange', Saughall Massie (see page ???????????). The cost of building the chapel was £698.

The first minister was the Rev. R. Lewis Powell from 1907-36. After the war, the population of Moreton grew rapidly and the church membership grew rapidly also. The chapel became too small, so it was decided to raise funds for a new chapel. There was plenty of room still on the original site that was bought in 1906. The memorial stone for the new chapel was laid on the 6th February, 1926 and the Chapel opened later that year; the total cost being £3,007. It was quite an achievement with wages being on average - four pounds a week. It was soon obvious that the new chapel was too small and that an extension would be necessary. On the 12th August, 1935, a meeting was held at which the Committee decided an extension was needed. Sadly, the man who had been the inspiration through all the changes, the Rev. R. Lewis Powell, died on the 2nd March, 1936. He was loved and admired by all the people of Moreton, not just church members, and he was missed greatly. On the 3rd November, 1936 a new minister was welcomed, namely Rev. H. Arfon Price. Twelve months later, on the 25th November, 1937, the new minister conducted the Dedication Service of the new extension and unveiled the beautiful memorial window to the late Rev. R. Lewis Powell. The extension cost £2,040 and the original chapel is now used as the Church Hall. The original front was extended in 1956. In its 88 year history, the Church has had five ministers - Rev. R. Lewis Powell 1907-36; Rev. H. Arfon Price 1936-50; Rev Alun Lewis, M.A. 1951-58; Rev. W. O. Jones 1959-65; and the Rev. Barrie J. Redmore, B.A. 1966 to the present day.

In its time, the church has had a Tennis Club that was situated in Alwyn Gardens; a Cricket Club that played on ground owned by a Mr Williams in Sandbrook Lane, a Horticultural Society, Scouts, Boys Brigade, a Drama Society, and is still a well-attended church.

The picture on the top left hand page dates from the 1910's. The one below just after it was built in 1926.

The picture above was also taken just after the extension was built in 1937. The one below is of the interior, before the extension was built approx 1927.

The Baptist Church started with a meeting of like-minded people in 1926 namely Mr. W. Holdsworth, Mr. J. E. Hendly and Mr. W. P. Williams. They initially worshipped at the Presbyterian Church, with it being the only Free church in the area. The three families used to meet at the home of Mr. & Mrs. Holdsworth in Rosslyn Drive, called 'Farsley'. The group slowly grew in size until one day in the summer of 1926, at a garden party held by Mr & Mrs. Holdsworth, they agreed to establish a Baptist Church in Moreton. The first official worship began there on Sunday evenings, amongst the first speakers in the Holdsworth drawing room, were Mr. F. J. Winchester of Egremont and Mr. Ellison, a retired missionary. A site was found on the corner of Doreen Avenue and Hoylake Road and was bought for £600 on the 27th may 1927 from a Mr. J. W. Jackson and Mr K. F. James, in the names of Mr. J. Bennett. Mr. J. H. Bourn, Mr. L. Doyle, Mr W. Holdsworth and Mr R. Parry on behalf of the Liverpool Baptist Union. The site was dedicated on the 1st October, 1927 and a short service was held to commemorate the occasion. Temporary headquarters were needed and found at the Victory Hall (now the British Legion) in Pasture Road. The first public service was held on the 2nd October, 1927. the hall could only be used on Sunday mornings and evenings as it was used for dances on Saturday nights. On Sunday mornings, the people were greeted with streamers and decorations hanging all around the hall. This made hard work until fate took a hand. In November 1928, the Victory Hall was declared unsafe, so the legion Hall was moved to Upton road (where Winston Grove is now - see page 17, Vol 1). the church services often had to be finished early, as other people wanted to use the hall. It was not until the 8th November 1930 that the congregation finally had a Church of their own. With the generous help of many of the members, they obtained a mortgage of £450 to build the church. The mortgage was finally paid on the 30th November, 1934, on the payment of £100 - a gift in memory of Dr. George Stansfield. It was soon found that more room was needed and a new chapel was proposed on the 3rd July, 1935. Mr. E. H. Wynn was in charge of the building fund. There was a quick response and £100 was donated by Mr. T. Parry, a further £100 through him and another £100 came from Mr. W. R. Minto. The foundation stones were laid on the 28th September, 1935 by Mr. J. F. Hindly on behalf of the church; Dr. F. B. Julian, President of the Liverpool Baptist Union, Mr. J. H. Bourn and Mr. T. Parry (represented by Mrs. E. Parry). The new Chapel was opened on the 11th April, 1938 by the Vice Moderator of the Lancashire and Cheshire Association. The new Chapel cost £1,577 - the final payment to clear the cost of the building was made on the 25th May, 1942. The Chapel was built by Sam Burrows and Sons. The original church was pulled down in 1965. By 1975 there was a need for a larger chapel as the congregation had grown to over two hundred. A new chapel was built in Doreen Avenue (at the back of the old one) at a cost of approximately £10,000. The original brick chapel is now used as a coffee and tea room.

The picture bottom left dates from September 1935 showing the laying of the foundation stone by Dr. F. B. Julian. The picture above shows the original building on the right of the picture. Below is the present building in Doreen Avenue taken in 1991.

The Gospel Hall in Old Maryland Lane had its origins in Kingsmead Caravan and Camping Field where several families belonged to the Plymouth Brethren. They held meetings in one or others tents and caravans-cum-bungalows. This was in the mid 1910's and the person responsible for arranging these early meetings was a Mrs. Bunner. By 1920, one of several Missionary's used to call in the summer months for two or three weeks at a time. One was Mr. Clark, another was Mr. Broadbent. Only a handful of people came but it was a start. With the help of Mr. Clark, they found a more permanent home in an old army hut in Carnsdale Road (then Durban Road). It was on the left hand side about halfway up - there was no water, toilets or heating so it was very cold in the winter time, even so the congregation slowly grew in numbers. By late 1929 the hut was falling down and was condemned. They then moved to the British Legion hut in Upton Road (see page 17 Vol 1). As the hut was used for dancing on Saturday nights, decorations were left hanging from the beams making life very difficult. By the late 1929/early 1930's, Mr. Gavin Hamilton, an Evangelical Preacher, who used to hold meetings in a large tent in Chadwick Street (where the Police Station now stands) became the driving force behind building a chapel in Moreton. With his guiding hand and encouragement, a meeting was held by the elders, and it was decided that they needed a more permanent home with no distractions. A site was offered to them for a nominal £50 in Old Maryland Lane, that was owned by the Ellis family whose daughter Bella was a member of the Chapel. By now, they were known as the Christian Brethren and collected amongst themselves £500. All the women gave their jewellery, and Mr. Morgan, a jeweller in Liscard, who was a member of the Liscard Chapel got the best price he could. The building of the Gospel Hall started on 30th April, 1932 at 3.15pm after an opening address by Mr Thomas on the laying of the first brick. It was originally to be an asbestos building but they changed their minds and decided to have a brick one and as a result ran out of money. They were left with a chapel without a roof. Mr Pearce, a builder from Heswall and a member of the Heswall Gospel Hall, came to their rescue and paid for the roof work and supplied the tiles for the roof. The church had its first service at 6.30pm on the evening of the 25th February, 1933. The pulpit came from a Baptist Church in Mold in 1971, paid for by Mr. Danny Evans in memory of his mother. The brothers Cyril and Ken Mates brought it to the Moreton Chapel in the back of a horse van and Mr John Waring put it together and polished it.

The original families that founded the Gospel hall were Messrs. A. L. Beed, Thomas Hyslop, A. E.Hayley, C. G. Mates, E. W. Robinson, P. Sheldon, F. Taylor. (Mr P. Sheldon owned and ran the Virginia Laundry in Seacombe).

The picture above is of a Chapel Outing in 1933. The names from left to right starting on the back row are

Back Row:
1 Danny George 2 Betty Mates (Davis) 3 Ken Mates 4 George Holford 5 Cyril Mates 6 Mrs Ashcroft
MiddleRow:
1 Olive Thorogood 2 3 Sissy Evens 4 Vera George 5
Bottom Row:
1 Ernie Pye 2 Doreen Ashcroft

The top picture left is of Gavin Hamiltons big marque tent in Chadwick St where the Police Station is now the picture dates from 1919. There was know Chadwick St then just a footpath to the site. Below is the laying of the Foundation Stone by Mr. Thomas on the 30th April 1932. The top picture on the right shows the inside of the hall in 1933 when it was opened and below the front taken at the same.

Above is a picture of Moreton Rectory, built in 1863, the same time as the Church by Mr. J. Sheriff of Upton. Unfortunately, the Rectory became so damp that it was uninhabitable and was pulled down in 1921. The Rector at the time was the Rev. W. J.Spink who had to move into a house in Glebelands Road until the new Rectory, on the corner of Dawpool Drive, was built in the 1930's.

Below shows Moreton's first brass band in 1899. It was run by the Christ Church until they had a disagreement with the Rev. Spink, who was disliked. The Band was later re-formed and again disbanded several years later after complaints by the local people of the noise they made. The instruments were sold to the Liverpool Childrens' Orphanage. They then formed the Albert Memorial Orphanage Band (see page 35).

On the facing pages are photographs of the Rectors of Christ Church from 1863 - 1969, with their names and the dates of their time there. The present day Reverend is Reverend R. A. Walton who took over from Rev. Smith in 1991. He in turn took over from Rev. Edwards in 1969 see right hand side.

The names from left to right back row are Joe Potter Matthews (the Conductor), Harry Wilson, Jack Roberts, Joe Stanley, Joe Goodwin, Jimmy Mack, Jack Potter, Wilf Smoith.
Middle Row: Harry Brassy, Tom Mutch, Don Garner, George Smith, Tom Potter, Joe Wilson (Coach & Horses Greensman), Tom Clark, Owen Stanley, bottom two not known.

1ST RECTOR
Rev. Matthew Fearnley M.A.
1863 – 1897

4th RECTOR
Rev. J. Edwards A.K.C.
1949 – 1969

2nd RECTOR
Rev. W.J. Spink M.A.
1897 – 1926

3rd RECTOR
Rev. C.E. Wormell B.A.
1926 – 1949

The picture above shows one of the two City Caterer's Cafes in Moreton. This one is on the corner of Leasowe Road/Pasture Road in about 1920 before the roads were raised and repaired. The building was used by many people in many various ways. It was first and foremost a cafe. On Sundays it was used as a Catholic Church until their own church was built on Upton Road in 1923. Also, during the week, part of it was used as a school. During the war time it was used as a factory where ammunition boxes were made. During and after the war, it was used by the Scouts. Finally, in the late 1950's it was pulled down - part of the foundation can still be seen.

The first priest to serve the growing community was Provost Barry from 1921 to 1923, who held his services in the cafe above. Canon Griffin came next from 1923 to 1930 - he served in the new church (near Marion Drive - see page 8 Vol. 1). He was held in high regard by the people and Griffin Avenue was named after him. Next came Father Peter Gerard from 1930 to 1939. He realised that there was a growing need for a school and organised 'Donkey Derby's' with the leading jockey's of the day such as Gordon Richards to name but one. This was so successful that the Sacred Heart School was built in 1934 at a cost of £10,000 and was opened by Bishop Moriarty. Next came Father Rees (later Monsignor Rees) from 1939 to 1983. He was known by just about everybody in Moreton. Then in quick succession came Father Monroe, Canon Walton, Father Tony. Father Brendan Hoban and Father Nick Kerns are at the church at the present time.

The picture on the facing page shows the opening of the new church that was built at a cost of £42,000. The amount that was outstanding was paid off by Monsignor Rees on his retirement in 1983. The Opening Ceremony attracted a large crowd, as can be seen on the facing page, on the 26th June, 1957. The Right Rev. John. A. Murphy presided at the opening together with the Bishop of Shrewsbury. The occasion was well-covered by all the local press and the Evening Express, for those who can remember it, did an extra special two-page coverage the following day. The picture below shows the Bishop blessing the outside of the church.

BRITISH MADE THROUGHOUT
olivetti
TYPEWRITERS
Phone CENtral
7744
(3 lines)
12. 15. 18. 23 & 27 inch CARRIAGES
ALL STYLES OF TYPE
JENKINSON'S
18/21 TITHEBARN ST., L'POOL 2

Evening Express

EXTRA SPECIAL

No. 26,742   LIVERPOOL, THURSDAY, JUNE 27, 1957   2½d.

Impressive scenes at the opening of . . .

MORETON'S NEW R.C. CHURCH

ABOVE: THE BISHOP OF SHREWSBURY KNEELS BEFORE THE ALTAR DURING THE SOLEMN BLESSING OF MORETON'S NEW CHURCH.

BELOW: THE PARISHIONERS RECEIVE BLESSING AS THE BISHOP LEAVES THE CHURCH OF THE SACRED HEART.

AT THE FOOT OF THE PAGE: SOME OF THE MANY PEOPLE WHO PAUSED TO WATCH THE IMPRESSIVE CEREMONY.

Methodism did not begin in Moreton until 1948. On 4th July, 1948 the first service was heard at the 'Church among the Trees' in Childwall Avenue, known as the Hillcrest Mission. It was on the plot of land that was at the back of Burrell Drive and at the end of Childwall Avenue. It was also known as Pastor Harris' Mission - he lived in Meadowbrook Road. Regular morning services started in July 1952 and on the 26th April, 1953 services were held in the newly-built hall in Pasture Road. The church itself was opened on the 18th September, 1954. These buildings were called the Poulton Road Memorial Church and cost £47,000 - the major part of which was met by the War Damage Compensation from the church in Seacombe.

Below are some of the leaders of Moreton Methodist Church, their names are, left to right, back row: Mr. E. Hughes, Mr. R. S. Griffith, Mrs. R. S. Griffiths, Rev. W. J. Besley, Miss N. Hughes and Mr. R. H. Dodd. Seated: Miss. J. Snelson, Mrs. N. Snelson, Mrs. A. E. Nicholson, Mrs. N. Whitehall and Mrs. L Fellowes. The picture dates from 1950.

The top picture shows a group of Sunday School children in 1949.

The Salvation Army first came to Moreton in the early 1910's and held open-air meetings on Moreton Shore. They later moved to one of the City Caterer's buildings on Pasture Road (see top picture on the right). The meetings were so well attended, it was decided to build their own hall. A site was chosen in Barnston Lane. It was built in October 1929 and opened the same month. The first leaders were Captain Parthouse and Lieutenant Late. The building is still standing (see picture below).

Fellowship House was built in the mid 1800's by a Mr. J. Sheriff for the Carlyle family (the Thomas Carlyle who was the great Scottish thinker). He also built Moreton Parish Church in Upton Road. The house was bought in 1911 by the Burden family who came from Liverpool. They had previously had a long association with Moreton through Mrs. Burdens grandfather. Mrs Burden was a suffragette and one of the founders of the Labour Party (then called the Independent Labour Party) She held a life-long belief in holidays for the working class, and very quickly put her belief into practice. Having a large amount of land, in the next year, 1912, she had three large bell tents and let it be known by word of mouth, that they were for rent at 2/6d a week (now 12-1/2p). It grew quickly into a total of eleven fields called Fellowship Field and numbered from one to eleven. Fellowship House and the first seven fields were situated where the present day Texaco Petrol Station is on Pasture Road opposite Premier Brands (once Cadbury's) main gate, and the surrounding Tarran Industrial Estate, named after the Prefabs that were there Fields 8 & 9 were situated where Kingsmead Road is, off Reeds Lane, and Fields 10 & 11 were on the corner of Pasture Road/Ditton Lane (see page 82, Vol 1). By the First World War, a lot of tents were replaced by caravans and small wooden bungalows, costing between £5 and £10. After the war, just about all the tents had gone, except for the odd one here and there. The returning soldiers used the money they were paid on demobilisation, to improve their homes and also extend them, as they had nowhere else to live. It was a hard life - there was no running water. The water was carried from one of two taps on each field. There were no bathrooms or toilets in the bungalows. The toilet was a small, square, wooden hut over a hole in the ground or placed over a ditch. They had no toilet paper, just newspaper torn into squares. By 1928 Moreton was getting a bad name and as Wallasey Corporation wanted more space to build houses, the bungalows were condemned. Mrs. Burden, together with several other people from the caravans, went to London to the House of Commons, to put their case to Mr. Arthur Greenwood, who was the Home Secretary. He advised that they do nothing to move the campers at the moment. The outcome of the discussion was the building of Pasture Avenue, Westway, Eastway, Ivy lane, part of Danger Lane, School Close, Eastway School and the start of Pasture Crescent. There are still some families living in the houses who came from the caravans. Most of the caravans that were movable and did not fall down, were taken to Talacre, Gronant, Prestatyn and other resorts in North Wales. A few caravans went to Lower Heswall. Mr. Jack Smith, with his horse 'Old Bobby', helped to move over seventy caravans. Other people who helped to move them were the Parkinson's, Coyne's and Brosters. It was the end of an era. Although Mrs. Burden still kept a few marquee tents until the late 1950's/early 1960's. She died in 1960. The land was sold off to become the present day petrol station. Many people who became well known in late life spent there early chilhood day on the Fellowship Fields. A young lady called Miss Bayforth who was better known as Bessie Braddock. The picture below shows part of Fellowship Field No. 2.

Fellowship No. 2 Field, Moreton.

Above is an advertising card for Fellowship House from the late 1910's, also from the same period below is Fellowship House with Mr & Mrs. Burden standing outside.

Both pictures on this page date from the 1910's and are of Fellowship Field. The top one shows the right hand side with the rear of Sunnyside - the brickworks' houses-below shows the left hand side.

Both these pictures date from the 1920's. The top one shows Fellowship Field No. 2 and the one Fellowship Field No. 4. The building on the left in the picture below was a Socialist Sunday School run by the Burden family. On the beams inside they had a motto God is Love, work to live then own the means by which you live.

The top picture dates from the late 1950's with Mrs. Burden standing in the doorway. The house and the grounds as can be seen from the picture were in a sad state of decline by then. The picture below taken in 1950 shows, from left to right, Mr & Mrs. Parry and Jill Parry, Alex Hurley, Reg Hurley and Pat Hurley. Both families came from Liverpool.

ACKNOWLEDGEMENTS

Bill Aspey
Andy Beed
Eric Knowles
Ken Hopkins
Kevin Cockroft
Jack Watling
Ces Smith (for his poem)
Stan Lampkin
George Bell
Jack Wagner
Tom Turner
Fred Smith
Mr. Mates
Mr. Sutton
Mrs. Pat Edwards
Mrs. Elma Davies
Mrs. Hoey
Mrs. Pat
Miss Marjorie Jeffrey
Mr & Mrs. Bridge
Mr & Mrs. Eric Johnson
Mrs. Sarginson
Mrs. Boardman
Owen Whitfield
George Munday

Mr. Bill Naylor

Wallasey Reference Library,
Earlston Road
Birkenhead Reference Library,
Borough Road
Liverpool Reference Library

and apologies to the people that we have forgotten to mention.

Volume 3 will contain : Moreton from the air
                       Moreton at War
                       Moreton Cross
                       Frank 'Tich' Mason (the jockey)
                       West Kirby R.A.F. Camp
                       The Hovercraft